GO TWEET YOURSELF

365 Reasons Why Twitter, Facebook, MySpace, and Other Social Networking Sites Suck

janelle randazza

AVON, MASSACHUSETTS

Published by
Adams Media, a division of F+W Media, Inc.
57 Littlefield Street, Avon, MA 02322. U.S.A.
www.adamsmedia.com

ISBN-10: 1-4405-0366-4
ISBN-13: 978-1-4405-0366-5

Printed in the United States of America.

J I H G F E D C B A

Library of Congress Cataloging-in-Publication Data
is available from the publisher.

This publication is designed to provide accurate and authoritative information with
regard to the subject matter covered. It is sold with the understanding that the publisher is not engaged in rendering legal, accounting, or other professional advice.
If legal advice or other expert assistance is required, the services of a competent
professional person should be sought.

—From a *Declaration of Principles* jointly adopted by a Committee of the
American Bar Association and a Committee of Publishers and Associations

Many of the designations used by manufacturers and sellers to distinguish their
product are claimed as trademarks. Where those designations appear in this book
and Adams Media was aware of a trademark claim, the designations have been
printed with initial capital letters.

This book is available at quantity discounts for bulk purchases.
For information, please call 1-800-289-0963.

Acknowledgments

Many thanks to those who selflessly and shamelessly aired their grievances about social networking (among other things), and helped keep me good and cynical when my predisposition toward optimism threatened the completion of this book. In no particular order, my gratitude goes out to: Mel and Amber Georgakopoulos, Burke Sampson, Stephanie Cornell, Amy Kucharik, Amy Mees, Emily Beaver, Liz Polay-Wettengal, Marya "Emdot" Figueroa, Chris Marstall, John Cotter, Elisa Gabbert, Paul McEvoy, Ed Meagher, Brigid Carroll Casellini, Andy Stochansky, Lisa Whynott, Keith Hastings, Betsy "Doily" Foley, Carlos Arboleda, Alicia Demirjian, Andy Fenenbock, Kevin McCarthy, Sara Ulnet, Chad and Kristina Harter Carlberg, Molly Scannell, Shauna Peck Slome, and Matthew Phillion. Many of you offered up your own social networking nightmares, allowing me to pass them off as my own in this book; I'm forever indebted to you. Very special thanks to Liam King; my parents John and Joanne, who did their best to brainstorm ideas despite rarely logging in to their shared Facebook account and being absolutely certain it is called "Faceplace"; and my brother Marc John Randazza. Your discontent is an inspiration, my dear brother.

Thank you to my blindingly talented editor, Wendy Simard. When the entire world gave me nothing but cricket chirps, your gleeful laughter at my sick sense of humor got me through. Thank you for your tireless and creative work on this project, and for everything else, my dear friend. Thanks to everyone else at Adams Media who made this book possible, especially publisher Karen Cooper, Brendan O'Neill, and designer Elisabeth Lariviere.

For Niamh Antoinette Sheedy and Natalia Antoinette Randazza: My favorite little girls on the planet. Social networking really can suck but you two never cease to rule.

Contents

PART 1

TWITTER: THE WHOLE WORLD, GONE TO THE BIRDS

PART 2

FACEBOOK: A FACE ONLY A MOTHER COULD LOVE

PART 3

EVERYTHING ELSE:
THE ONLINE OUTCASTS

Introduction

I hope you're sitting down as you read this, because I'm about to deliver a shock of biblical proportions. No one cares if you're going for a walk, eating lunch, playing the banjo, or taking a nap. And we care even less if you tell us in a mere 140 characters. Somewhere between the time Facebook became a club even Great-Aunt Suzy wanted membership in and Twitter went pandemic, we began to exalt the mundane and worship the inane.

We have entered a new age of excess, only with the world's economy in dumps we're turning toward an overabundance of blather, in the form of Insipid Status Update, over-posting of photos, over-liking of posts, and self-important drivel about what color socks we plan to wear and what brand of ketchup we prefer on our fries. The more we talk, the less we listen and the more Facebook friends, Twitter followers, and LinkedIn connections we acquire the greater the chance that any sliver of meaningful contact we could forge will get lost in the din of nudges, pokes, prods, and virtual two-steps.

Social networking has become a game that no one can win as we try to eek an iota of meaning from where there is none through silly status posts, and insincere cyber gift-giving.

Let's be perfectly clear people, I don't want a virtual drink, hug, or pet pterodactyl, nor do I want social interactions that are limited to 140 characters—and neither should you! Hopefully the following 365 reasons will convince you that social networking is akin to a zombie invasion that is eating all of our brains, leaving us as vapid nodes who somehow believe there is importance in telling the world we're buying a carton of milk.

Consider it my mission to motivate (or shame) you into getting a life—a real life, not the virtual variety. If that doesn't work, at the very least you'll have something to tweet about tomorrow.

PART 1

TWITTER: THE WHOLE WORLD, GONE TO THE BIRDS

Everybody gets so much information all day long that they lose their common sense.

—Gertrude Stein

Chapter 1

You Are What You Tweet

1 > Thought blogs were self-indulgent? Try microblogging!

If a tweet goes out in a forest, and no one sees it, does it make a sound? When your thoughts or tweets or twits—or whatever you want to call them—get pushed further and further down your friends' update feed with each passing second, it's not connecting you to anyone. You're just yammering to yourself and everyone is so preoccupied with the sound of their own tweets that they don't care what you have to say—you're in a virtual middle school bathroom and you're surrounded by self-absorbed cheerleaders. It's as if all this tweeting is a territorial call, as opposed to a mating—or friendship—call.

You know who the most social of all birds are? Penguins. That's right. Why is that? Because penguins know how to hang, how to take time out to share a fish—and how to listen. No obsessive tweeting goes on in Antarctica. We could learn a thing or two from a penguin.

Twit Lingo

Twitterize (verb): Using peer pressure to convert a new Twitter user into a Twit.

2 > The anatomy of a Twit

I didn't think birds got rabies, but Twitter has proven science wrong. Get a die-hard Twit in a room and she'll start pecking you on the skull about the importance of Twitter like a raccoon that wants your lunch or a Jehovah's Witness dead set on saving your soul. There is no stopping these Twits. They bang on your door and damn you to hell if you don't convert to their cult. I know that when we refuse to believe in Twitter the terrorists win, but Twitter was founded in 2006; if 60 percent of its users *still* don't get it, I'm going to go out on a limb and say it's not working.

3 > Twitter can't even figure out the point of Twitter

If Twitter is so revolutionary, than why can't even Twitter figure out what the point of it is? It's as if Paris Hilton wrote their mission statement. Don't believe me? Check out Twitter's "Why" page, which explains "why" the service is so useful. The first bullet point—in an alarmingly succinct three-point list—reads, and I quote: "Eating soup? Research shows that moms want to know." Eating soup? What does that even mean? There is more meaning and depth in episodes of *90210* than in Twitter's self-stated purpose.

4 > The fragmented life

The @reply feature is the only thing about the site that allows for interactivity. But if you're going to have a twenty-point discussion—complete with the occasional LOL thrown in there for good measure—does the whole world need to see it? And if you are thoroughly convinced the whole world **does** need to see it, could you at least let us see both sides of the conversation so we have some semblance of a clue as to what you're talking about? (Twitter's fault, not yours—but I have to yell at someone.)

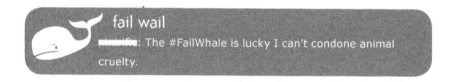

fail wail

██████: The #FailWhale is lucky I can't condone animal cruelty.

5 > One of the founders goes by the name of "Biz"

The company was cofounded by a guy who wants you to call him "Biz." And it's not like his parents played a cruel joke on him and we should all be nice. The guy's name is Christopher! Some might say that Christopher is a mouthful, but aren't there other, more suitable nicknames for Christopher? Like, I don't know . . . how about "Chris"? Or if you hate the name Chris, why not try Topher, like Topher Grace. How does "Biz" even fit in there? If insisting people call you Biz isn't pompous, I don't know what is. There's another guy in charge, Evan Williams, but his name is pretty vanilla.

6 > And while we're on the subject of silly names . . .

It would have been way more fun if they named Twitter something like Twatter. Just think of all the fun we could have had if all the users were called Twats. And when you tweet they called it twatting. Way more fun. Gets you thinking. Puts a smile on your face. Twitter should have had me in on those first business-planning meetings. People would have been way more enthusiastic about adopting my idea and I bet there even would have been more opportunities for ad revenue! It would have ruled.

7 > I'm allowed to make fun of Biz Stone twice

I think he can take it. Stone was quoted in *New York* magazine as saying, "Twitter is not about the triumph of technology. It's about the triumph of the human spirit." Aw, that's a nice sentiment, Biz. Thing is, I can't help but feel like my spirit is shackled to an electronic device every time I tweet. I'm not so sure my spirit is triumphing. Maybe my iPhone is, but my spirit? Not so much.

8 > The media's crush on tweeting

Maybe it's newspapers' way of trying to stay relevant as they all go the way of the Dodo, but they *really* got it bad for Twitter. The *New York Times* has gone so far as to elevate tweeting to "a sort of philosophical act. It's like the Greek dictum to 'know thyself,' or the therapeutic concept of mindfulness." Perhaps, but I can't help but think there are better ways to know thyself than by updating your Twitter feed, where self-realization is bookended between one friend's broadcast that they're buying a dozen donuts and another's declaration that he's about to take his dog out for a poop.

Insipid (CELEb) Status Update

BabyGirlParis (Paris Hilton): Just had an amazing lunch and tan at the pool. Back in my beautiful room getting ready for another fun-filled night :)

9 > Lean on me . . . when you're not strong

The biggest problem I have with Twitter is that it doesn't really work on its own, which is probably why 60 percent of all tweeters never return to their account after signing up for the service. With only a 40 percent saturation rate, Twitter has created a web-based product that doesn't really work without assistance from a third-party app, like TweetDeck or Twhirl. Without them Twitter is labor intensive and non-user-friendly. Why doesn't Twitter just create something on their home page that works? As it stands, it's like arriving at a speakeasy without a password. If a third party is doing it, why can't Twitter? And that way all those moms with dead accounts could get their important soup updates and stuff.

10 > The third-party fiasco

Because Twitter forces you to use third-party apps to really make it useful, there is always the risk that even if Twitter isn't down, the app might be. And if both are up, sometimes it's simply a problem of the two not connecting. Thank you, Twitter, for creating a cluster you-know-what for us to deal with. And so there you are, waiting for the app to come online again, feeling totally screwed because people are posting soup updates . . . and you're missing the whole thing.

11 > Wasn't *The Birds* a horror movie?

I know they're trying to push the cute-and-friendly factor, but the Twitter icons creep me out. Have you ever gotten to the suspended account page? A cavern-eyed owl appears, looking as if it's been on a week-long bender and the only way to make it through is to stare you down. Hitchcock liked to expose the terror that can lurk in the commonplace, so it's pretty fitting that we have these disturbing little birds lurking at every corner, waiting to strike.

Don't even get me started on what happens if you download TweetDeck, which offers up a dull, robotic tweet sound effect at every update. And what if you start following more than twenty regular tweeters? The eerie din of the flock is enough to make even the Master of Suspense shudder.

12 > The "celebrity" endorsements on the home page

I even get the feeling that the endorsers of Twitter don't really like Twitter all that much. The company's founders have been hanging in the Silicon Valley for some time, so you think they could've bribed their friends with better endorsements than, "I really like Twitter," which is the über-enthusiastic endorsement from a senior manager at Amazon. Twitter must have been *pretty* desperate for endorsements to post that on their home page. Just because you like something doesn't mean you use it with any frequency or recommend it to friends. I happen to like peanut butter, but that doesn't mean I'm going to eat it every day.

13 > "The Telegraph System of 2.0"

That is a pretty strong endorsement by Nicholas Carr, an author and technologist, who seems to see great potential in the power of tweets. I can certainly see the comparisons, only there is one major difference: The telegraph was both a practical and commercial success. Twitter? Well, as of today, it ain't generating a red cent.

14 > More like the co-dependent partner of 2.0

"I'm watching TV!" "I'm going to the store!" "I'm totally going to buy that gallon of milk!" Twitter is the web service for the emotionally needy. Imagine if this were real life. I don't know anyone who would willingly want to know every heartbeat and bodily function of anyone at any time the way Twitter allows you to. Think about it: Do you really need to be in touch with everyone, every second of every day? Do you really need the up-to-the minute updates of what all of your friends are doing at every second? I think what you need is a nice, long walk. (Leave your Crackberry at home.)

15 > Don't call me a follower

Can't they call us something a little more dignified? Like a connection, or a groupie or something? Being a follower makes me feel like I've joined up with the Maharishi, which gets right back to the whole point of Twitter being the social media outlet for the emotionally needy.

16 > The ADD-inducing service

I thought I could handle it, but I can't. They're going to need to create some Ritalin-like drug for people to deal with Twitter. It's almost like ADD and OCD all rolled into one and it's wigging me out. The problem is, once you sign up, you begin to think about stuff you never thought about before. Stuff like:

"I wonder if James is going to eat that donut" and "We're all having cocktails but I've checked Twitter thirty times in the past hour and they haven't tweeted about how much fun they're having with me. Everyone hates me and no one wants to be my friend." I think I know what's going on. The Twitter founders are all disgruntled adults who grew up with ADD and this is a government plot to train the minds of the masses to have ADD too. Place your online order for Ritalin now. It's your only hope for survival.

17 > It's time for a Twitter intervention when . . .

Don't look now, but there's a new Twit on the block and he's dying to use the site to show how important he is. Oh look! He just learned hashtags. And now my TweetDeck is going berserk because he has uploaded at least thirty-seven sayings that are #FunnierInLithuanian. I should certainly hope these are funnier in Lithuanian, because none of this stuff is funny in English. That is the power of Twitter. (And you thought it was just about soup.)

18 > Twitter is a total spazz

You know who Twitter is? Twitter is that girl you went to school with who would bust into class and say, "You are NEVER going to believe this." Then she'd give you two sentences before the teacher walked in. Then during the course of class she'd think better of giving you the whole story, so all you'd have is an unsubstantiated panic over your best friend and boyfriend sitting at McDonald's together. Case in point? Swine flu. The "swine flu" meme has proved that misinformed people, armed with a platform to broadcast their fears, can easily incite more fear and misinformation thanks to pathological status updates. Kinda like an errant virus. Ironic, isn't it?

Insipid Status Update

@~~███████~~: The people who say I'm arrogant and shallow don't see me when I'm at home with my wife. Did I mention that she's a former swimsuit model?

19 > Fame and glory in the Twittosphere

It's really weird when you post a tweet that "thanks" your one hundredth follower. Especially when your list of followers counts nonhumans, like Whole Foods, JetBlue, and Palm Inc. Just because people follow you, it doesn't mean they're your fans. It doesn't mean you need to give an Oscar acceptance speech.

20 > Why on earth does Virgin America want to follow me?

Don't they have someone more important to follow, like Paula Abdul or somebody? They're following more than 15,000 people, why do they want to follow me? I get a ton of requests like this—from galleries, jewelers, news organizations. These businesses don't care what you have to say. They don't want to make friends. They just want to hawk their wares. Just another reason why Twitter is tearing us apart as opposed to bringing us together. Sure, VA, you can follow me. Just know that my updates are few and far between these days, and I get the distinct feeling you don't care what kind of soup I like. . . .

21 > When regular folks want to be Ashton Kutcher

So, you think you're an insta-celebrity because you have 10,000 followers? What some people won't do for their fifteen minutes of fame. These people believe the path to fame and glory is to rack up followers. And their pleas to get noticed couldn't be sadder. Every single one of them thinks she's going to get on the Ellen DeGeneres Show. I know this because I got twelve follower requests just this morning. I'm sure they are all awesome people who really have lots of important things to say in 140 characters, but considering how little I care about their quest to have the most followers of other Twits, I'm sure Ellen cares even less.

22 > Twitter quitters

I've said it before and I'll say it again: 60 percent of all Twits sign up and never return. So it's likely you have a wasteland of followers who don't give a hoot about what you say—because they don't have *any idea* you've been saying it! Your carefully crafted 140-character witticisms have been falling on deaf ears. Which makes me wonder: They've been without Twitter for months, and they seem to be doing okay. Does that mean I'd be okay if I never came back either?

23 > Inspiring the stupid

In real life we've been taught to think before we talk, but in Twitter, it's all about quantity, not quality, folks. Twitter has inspired people to talk about the stupid and to talk about it with greater frequency than you would have ever thought possible. And you can't ever get away from the torrent of stupidity because it pops up on your laptop and on your cell phone and the next thing you know it's chirping at you so insistently you feel like you're stuck in the parakeet cage at the pet store.

Insipid Status Update

@██████████: Girl at the gym was checking me out, I could tell she wanted me. A Philly 8, but she had sweaty arm pits. I don't date girls that sweat.

24 > If I want to tweet, I'll tweet, don't nudge me

The nudge function is what will ultimately cause me to lose my mind. Get this: If you have to take a few days off to hang with the kids and you haven't had time to post on Twitter, they have created a function to make sure you don't forget about the inane world of Twits you left behind. They have actually created a function for people to prod you to post more. It's called "nudging." Silence is golden, people—how about we give it a try?

25 > Cutesy names

Twitter, tweeting, twits, and twats: Please don't try to make a lexicon out of this Twitter. What's worse is the whole Twitionary, which encourages people to neologize new Twitterisms, making us all talk like we're the progeny of Elmer Fudd. Like "Twaffic," which means to Twitter while you're in traffic. This word should not even exist! Do not Twitter in traffic. Pay attention to the road and put the cell phone down! Unfortunately, Rainn Wilson seems to endorse this behavior, as evidenced in a recent tweet: "Boom, new word. Driving while texting = 'drexting'. Done. #drexting" . . . so sad.

26 > Nonthreaded conversations

You know, I'm really trying to be open-minded and like you, Twitter, but you make it so hard. I'm on this thing, trying to connect with my friends, but I can't figure out what anyone is talking about and, if I don't log in for a day, I've lost track of my conversations. Twitter needs threads—or branches or bird houses or whatever they want to call it to make them feel better. Threads are important in conversation, as they help you keep track of what has been said. With Facebook, you have that glorious Wall-to-Wall button so you can see a threaded conversation between two people, but you can't on Twitter. And that completely sabotages the real reason why people social network in the first place: stalking. No thread means you can't spy on other people and tweet-stalk them. Or Twalk them.

27 > Twindecision

Not only does Twitter not understand the point of their service conceptually, they don't understand it practically. They're like confused squirrels trying to cross the street. They should call their site Faker because they keep faking us out, trying one thing, taking it back, then trying it again. For example, the @reply fiasco. They just decided to get rid of it and then they faced such an uproar that they almost immediately backpedaled. How about thinking things through for a second and just allowing for a privacy feature in discussions? That's right—when too many people want to start a discussion with Oprah, we could just hide them! A logical idea, you might say. So why haven't they done that?

Insipid Status Update

28 > Twitting, Twatting, and hacking

Oh rad, I just found out Twitter stalkers can hack my cell texts. And this isn't the fun kind of stalking, which you do behind a computer monitor with a pint of New York Super Fudge Chunk on your lap. This is real live stalking—active stalking—which takes place out of doors. And that's scary! Apparently, if you tweet by cell phone those gross, creepy, real-life stalkers can get your GPS coordinates and, with the right software, find out exactly where you are. See! I told you this was a Hitchcock movie!

Twit Lingo

Twhacked (verb): A hacked Twitter—e.g., you got twhacked!

29 > Disconnecting to connect

The whole Twitter interface blows. My biggest beef? I'm on the page of someone I'm following and I like what they have to say. Can I just reply to them? No. I cannot. Why? Because Twitter is a bossy bastard. Unless you have a TweetDeck or something similar, Twitter makes you go all the way back to your page if you want to post to said follower's page. That's like trying to have a conversation with someone; they say something interesting, then you walk into another room, pick up the phone, and call them to tell them they're funny. Hmm . . . seems unnecessarily labor intensive when I put it that way, doesn't it?

30 > Twitter: tag line

"What are you doing?" Sure, it's short, sweet, and simple, but they couldn't come up with something better? How much did they pay their marketing team to come up with that one?

31 > It spreads like the plague

And speaking of catchy—this thing is spreading like the Spanish flu. With nearly 6 million users and counting, Twitter obliterated its first year's growth rate by 900 percent and is moving like a pestilence across the globe. And just like a pandemic, you see it suddenly infecting the least likely of friends and acquaintances—people you thought would be immune. It's like something out of a bad sci-fi movie where perfectly intelligent people suddenly turn into Twitting drones without the talent, social acumen, or attention span to say anything beyond 140-character snippets. As if we weren't all dumb enough, now Twitter has helped us to become both dumb and socially inept.

32 > The news media is starting to get creepy

We get it. The news media loves to talk about Twitter. It has now become mainstream practice for sites of all types, from politics to music to economics, to tweet. Heck, even highbrow publications like the *New Yorker* and *Harper's* tweet. Not a week passes without some overeager trend piece on how awesome Twitter is. I find myself wishing for the days when Britney Spears would flash her va-jay-jay just so the news would cover something besides how awesome Twitter is.

33 > Twitter style guide

You have GOT to be kidding me. A style guide exists for 140 characters? You mean to tell me there is a whole book on how to write in 140 characters and it only focuses on style? Dude, when you're trying your hardest to fit a snippet of important info into a cranny of space, style goes out the window.

Insipid Status Update

@█████: This morning three people received a round of applause at breakfast: the bride, the groom, and me.

34 > Second most Twitter-happy nation is Japan

Is anyone surprised that Japan loves Twitter and is the second most adoptive nation? Twitter is the closest thing most people will ever get to having their very own reality show, so it's really no coincidence that, with all of the bizarre reality shows that come out of Japan, the attention-loving culture was bound to latch on to what Twitter has to offer. Although, I must say, watching the Japanese dress up as "human Tetrises" is far more fun for me than following them on Twitter. But maybe something is lost in translation?

35 > Twitter journalism?

We are now starting to hear the terms: "Twitter journalism" and "Twitter criticism." The problem with Twitter journalism is what is inherently wrong with Twitter as a communication tool beyond anything more than "will be home at 6 P.M." Those 140 characters can only provide skeletal snapshots of a situation. Worse, these snapshots are difficult to follow; if a journalist Twitters you're bound to lose half of their info beneath sixteen other tweets from friends making soup.

36 > Avatar hell

Why is it so darn hard to load an avatar on this site? It takes days for an avatar to show up; don't even get me started on what happens when you want to change your avatar. Basically, it's not enough that Twitter is making us illiterate and socially awkward. It won't stop until its 19.1 million users are nameless, faceless, tweeting nodes.

37 > Images + Feed = Disaster!

Does Twitter even want me on Twitter? The Twitter interface basically takes the Internet back into the Dark Ages and, as far as photos or graphics are concerned, makes it impossible for you to gracefully post images in your feed. Clunky, crappy, crude: This is the wave of the future?

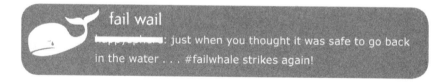

fail wail

@happyophelia: just when you thought it was safe to go back in the water . . . #failwhale strikes again!

38 > Incredible shrinking tweets!

I believe the point is for Twitter to hold on to all of your old tweets in perpetuity, but that just doesn't seem to be happening. Tweets can vanish without warning, leaving you totally tweetless. And with so many people tweeting, being tweetless is akin to being pantless.

TWIT STAT

Despite significant growth in Twitter accounts, 53 percent of registered users have no followers.

39 > Let's start a revolution!

Come on everyone! Let's start a movement—with a Twition! Sure, sign your name away to a cause that is best described in no more than 140 characters. What? You say you'd like to know a little bit more about a cause before you get behind it? But that would mean we'd actually have to share information. This is about creativity, man. Stop being so uptight. Your need for more information is harshing my mellow.

40 > Twitter is not a singles lounge

Follow me—fine; pursue me—no. Twitter is not the place to pick up women. And, for chrissake, don't ask me to tell you about myself. How am I supposed to tell you about myself in 140 characters or less? Unless, of course, there's not much you want to know.

41 > As if Match.com wasn't opaque enough

Flirt140.com, the Twitter dating site is truly a divine idea. Because when I've done online dating I've always felt the main problem was that I knew **too much** about the guy before I met him. I'm particularly enamored by the tagging feature, which lets you search by tags to find exactly the perfect mate. For example, HornyTron just tagged himself as "husband." Well, between the name and the promise within the tag, I'm sold!

Chapter 2

Blah, Blah, Blah . . .
But Keep It Brief, Dammit

42 > Who decided 140 was the magic number?

So this 140-character limit is allegedly there to "inspire creativity," claims he of the awesome and nonpretentious nickname. How is it more creative to turn the word "for" into "4" and the word "you" into "u" or the sentences "That is extremely funny. Your propensity for humor is both charming and beguiling" into "LOL"? If Oscar Wilde were alive, I think he'd have a few choice words to say to you. Sorry Biz, your 140-character limit doesn't inspire creativity at all—it just inspires really bad spelling.

Insipid Status Update

@██████: I just finished putting together something really cool. I won't tell you more about it but you should just know what a bad ass I am.

43 > Twitter makes you write like a hormonal teenager

Suddenly I find myself writing that I have loved Duran Duran's music 4-eva. I text that I'll TTYL and, just last week, without even realizing it, I told someone—out loud—I was having dinner with my BFF. No, I didn't say "my best friend forever"; I said, "my BFF." I don't know what's wrong with me. I went to college. I even went through the requisite existential poet phase, so I can assure you I know how to spell out "forever" and I have the tenacity to tell someone that I will "talk to you later." It's not that I'm lazy, I've just reverted to my high school ways. Twitter does this to you.

44 > A little birdie told me . . .

Speaking of high school, tweeting almost feels like the modern-day equivalent of passing notes in the school cafeteria. Your boss is forcing you to tweet, so what's the harm in quickly tweeting your friend about the cute bartender she should meet, while you're sitting in a dull presentation, Crackberry in hand? The best part? You never have to read it in front of the whole class because, really . . . the whole class could read it anyway if they wanted to.

....

Twit Lingo
Twishing (verb): Phishing on Twitter, e.g., He Twished my password!
....

45 > Who the f*#% counts characters when they type?

Don't cut me off! I'm talking here! You know, Biz, limiting me to 140 characters gives me an acute case of ADD. I just want to talk to my friends, but you keep cutting me off! You know what I think? I think you must be a really bad listener. I know guys like you; you just want to stuff us into a birdcage so we simmer down. Well joke's on you because I know why the caged bird sings! It's because some jerk told her to shut up after she tweeted 140 characters.

46 > It takes 171 characters for Twitter to explain what Twitter is

If you want to inspire creativity in your denizens, why not do it by setting an example? Twitter describes itself as "A service for friends, family, and co-workers to communicate and stay connected through the exchange of quick, frequent answers to one simple question: What are you doing?" Want to know how long that explanation is? 171 characters! Seems to me you should have to trim 31 letters and spaces from that bad boy.

Insipid Status Update

@▓▓▓▓▓▓▓: If you weren't on Twitter in 2007 you are NOT an authority on social media. At all.

47 > Sadly, your account does NOT come with an editor

I know this is going to come as a shock to all of you, but Paris Hilton is not the worst speller on the planet, as I thought she would be. Sadly, I am following people who, on a bad day, come pretty close to losing the Paris Hilton All-Collegiate Spelling Bee. And don't get me started on grammar. In real life you think people know the difference between "their" and "there"— sadly, because of the nature of Twitter, the truth comes out in mobile posts, exposing your friends as the kids whose best class was . . . woodshop.

48 > Repeat tweets

Hate to break it to you, folks. When you post a million tweets you aren't Twittering, you're e-mailing. Follow-up tweeters are cheaters. If you're going to tweet, you need to start playing by the rules. I get all OCD counting characters and then some Twitter Cheater goes on for a million posts to get his thoughts out? Uh, I don't think so. You take that follow-up tweet off your feed and keep your thoughts to 140 characters, just like everyone else. There's no room for a Chatty Cathy here at this party!

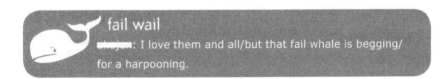

fail wail

▆▆▆▆▆: I love them and all/but that fail whale is begging/ for a harpooning.

49 > Entire books, dedicated to Twitter

What you're holding in your hands notwithstanding, how is it that something born of brevity has books coming out about it as well as manuals on how to use it? The whole point of Twitter, allegedly, is the simplicity and the pithiness of it. So how is it that it warrants dozens of books on the subject most of which run upward of 250 pages? It's obviously time to break out the darn Chewbacca defense because, people, this does not make sense.

50 > Tweets of depth

Let's get realistic here. They call it a tweet for a reason. If we think of a real tweet, they are light, and high-pitched, and uplifting. If they wanted you to say something deep they'd call it a Tsunami or a Tectonic Shift. Short. Sweet. Tweet. We just want a little taste. Just a little insight. So why some people have to make tweeting something it's not is beyond me. Deep Tweeters of the world, you know who you are. Stop trying to give weight to something that can't bear it. No need to be deep. Twitter wants you to be shallow, so if you're going to tweet you might as well give in.

51 > Wouldn't a text work just fine?

When was the last time you saw a tweet that 100 people needed to see? And, if 100 people did need to see it, wouldn't it have been a topic that required more than 140 characters' worth of information? I have friends who use Twitter to drive traffic to their blogs, which seems like a great idea in theory, but didn't we already have a much more organized way of getting information, which was an e-mail blast?

52 > This is sensory overload

How much social media can one person handle before it makes them anti-social? And before they cease to care? All this sensory overload is giving me PTSMD. Yes, that's right, it's Post-Traumatic Social Media Disorder.

....

Twit Lingo

Twithead (noun): Somebody who is full of twit.

....

53 > Aliens don't tweet

With all of the hundreds of alien abductees telling their stories, not one has reported seeing an alien tweeting. And everyone knows aliens are from the future doing really important scientific work. Unless they are stuffing Tweet-Decks into those anal probes, I don't see much future for Twitter. Also, it should be noted that Nostradamus never predicted anything about Twitter. Which leads me to believe this thing is totally doomed to fail.

54 > Just when you thought Twitter couldn't be more shallow

Nothing is more insincere than an auto-reply thank-you note. I'd rather get nothing at all! Don't tell me your goal is to connect with people when you've set up an auto-reply to thank me and then to request to follow me. It's like dating a guy who gives the same necklace to every woman he dates. It's a gift that is insincere. Come on, guys, don't cheapen what we have here. If you don't want me to call you in the morning, then just don't say anything when I follow you around. I'll get the picture. Promise.

Insipid Status Update

@▨▨▨▨▨▨: Off to lunch with the ex soon. My breakups are always dramatic but then my ex's always become my BFFs. Guess no one can quit me. :0)

55 > The "Shorties"

The Shorty Awards honor "the world's top Twitterers for their ability to write great content with 140 characters or less." Speaking of great content, don't they mean 140 characters or fewer? And let me point something out here: 140 characters don't make up content. They make up a tagline.

Chapter 3

The Twittersphere Time-Suck (or, How to Avoid Adult Activities)

56 > Trust me. No one cares that you [insert boring-ass task here]

I really didn't need to know that you just took your dog for a walk. I mean, it's awesome and all, but you take your dog for a walk every day. At least three times a day. This is not groundbreaking news. Just like it wasn't groundbreaking news that you bought a carton of orange juice. I suppose it's good that Twitter is making you take note of the little things in life, but please, don't drag us all down the path of inane self-discovery with you. I have enough inane thoughts running through my own head on a daily basis; I don't need yours to cause interference.

57 > Go ahead. Spend an hour crafting a witty post (that no one cares about)

Okay, I guess I'm talking to myself here. But you know that half of all Twits do this, and you don't want to be left looking like a moron. So you type in a little something, get up to get some coffee, come back, rethink it—you turn into a rabid revisionist, thinking you're James Joyce or something. Nothing but absolute perfection will do. And you know what's worse? No one is going to read what you so painstakingly crafted because within two minutes twelve posts about soup will appear after yours, pushing it all the way down the page. And you can't get that hour of your life back, pal. Consider yourself warned.

(CELEB)

Insipid ^Status Update

> **@JohnCMayer:** I love how some dudes hate me for dating their fantasy girl, as if they were going to if I hadn't.

58 > Slow as f#@*, but you'll *still* wait for the update

Something that doesn't make sense: Those that tend to be more technologically inclined choose Firefox over, say, Safari. And people who are more technologically inclined tend to use Twitter. So, why is it that Firefox and

Twitter don't seem to mesh? Why is it that the textbox is . . . So. Freaking. Slow. When you combine the two? Type. Watch nails grow. Wait. Type. Watch nails grow. Rinse. Repeat.

Twit Lingo

Twitfession (noun): A confession made on Twitter.

---

59 > You're stuttering again

Just wait a second folks. I know Twitter is slow as f#@*, but if you just give it a second, your update *will* appear. Promise. No need to post again. But if you find that you're starting to stutter, do us all a favor and delete the five repeats you just posted. Because no one needs to hear time and time again about how Adam Lambert was robbed on American Idol.

60 > Call me Ishmael

. . . because me and the Fail Whale, we seem to be best buds. Why is this site always down? Well, the Twitter Developer's blog says it's because Twitter wasn't built to be a messaging system—it was built "with the technologies and practices that are more appropriate to a content management system." But the Twitter website says it's a service for people to "communicate and stay connected through the exchange of quick, frequent messages." So . . . Twitter is arguing with itself? Okay, so—let me get this straight—the developers are saying the technology they use isn't consistent with the purpose of the product. And who is supposed to resolve this issue? Obama?

Insipid Status Update

@███████: ok poop is coming out.

61 > I thought this was IM

Twitter is IM, only without the instant gratification of actually having a conversation. Ever notice how the whole Web 2.0 deal started with bringing us together and now it's got us talking to ourselves? As though IM wasn't impersonal enough, Twitter had to take the idea one step further and pull us farther apart. It's perfect, really. And it truly fills a niche. It's like IM for the introvert.

62 > Direct messages

Awesome, one more e-mail account for me to check. I have one for work, one for personal life, one for Facebook, one for MySpace, one for LinkedIn, one for Flickr, and now one for Twitter. Why are you doing this to me, Twitter? I have to sign up with a freakin' e-mail address; can't you just allow people to send to that with an alias or something? And guess how many characters they allow you. Give up? 140. So basically, this is just a tweet that I have to click through to get—because it really serves no other function. You can't send out a message to a handful of people; you can't attach anything; can't use HTML. It's just one more opportunity for me to miss a message from someone.

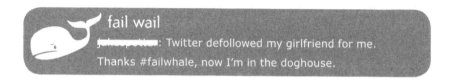

fail wail

_____: Twitter defollowed my girlfriend for me. Thanks #failwhale, now I'm in the doghouse.

63 > Where the heck do I e-mail you?

And on that note, how do I get in touch with people now? Not only does no one pick up the phone anymore—no one seems to be on e-mail either. Everyone is stuck on the sound byte of the moment. First it was texting and now it's tweeting. All I know is I want to get in touch with my friends but it seems the more you want to make a connection, the further away you get. Am I supposed to be using Twitter to invite you to parties? Is anybody listening? Is this thing on? I'm overwhelmed.

64 > Twitter hell on your cell

Unless you're some sexual deviant who always keeps your cell in your front pocket and on vibrate, getting Twitter sent to your cell is the worst idea ever.

Why? Because you CANNOT delete your messages fast enough. One of these days someone you follow is going to get on some hashtag kick and send out thirty updates in one day. And that's when you are screwed.

65 > Public access to courtrooms

Hmmm . . . something smells off here. Sure it's great to get real time, blow-by-blow updates on how justice prevails (one would hope), but I'm thinking the downsides might end up overshadowing the upsides. We already complain that journalism has gotten sloppy, and with no time for reporters to dig deep to give context and background of a case, it seems we're endorsing clumsy reporting. Let's just call it what it is, a race to get to the finish line first, no matter what the consequences are—and no matter what fact you accidentally leave out in the end. Free access to our justice system is great, but don't hide behind the First Amendment when what we are really talking about is slimy sensationalism.

TWIT STAT

As of December 2008, 11 percent of online American adults said they used a service like Twitter or another service that allowed them to share updates about themselves or to see the updates of others.

66 > Philanthropic tweets

Cool, let's use Twitter to accomplish something for the greater good. I'm all for it! But you have to wonder, is Twitter the best means of doing so? When organizations use Twitter to raise funds, are they really help-ing spread the mission of the organization and enlighten people as to why they need to help? Yes, philanthropy is about giving, but isn't it also about being more connected to a greater cause? By keeping everything to 140 characters, we allow people to give without actually thinking about what's wrong in the world. This also means that *anybody* with a cause can solicit funds—that's right, even the folks behind Operation Eat More Chocolate Cake. (Why didn't I think of that??)

....

Twit Lingo

Benetwit (verb): When Tweeps get together and twit for charity.

....

67 > No hide option—you either see them or you don't

Something Twitter could learn from Facebook? The ability to HIDE. Some-times I want to follow a person, just so I can occasionally keep track of what they're up to. But some of those people aren't people I want to follow on a daily basis. Besides, what if I have a temper tantrum or something and I just don't want to see them for a couple of days. Twitter is like the boyfriend who gives you an ultimatum (furthering my argument that Twitter is needy): All or nothing, bitch.

68 > When good people overtweet

This is when it gets hard. You used to like the person, until you found out that—while they're perfectly polite in the read world—in the Twittosphere they never shut up. A hashtag one minute and a retweet the next, these people are relentless. What to do? Call an intervention, or just step away slowly. Really, no choice is the right one. They have to first want to help themselves. Until that happens, there's nothing you can do.

Insipid Status Update

@j————————: I'm eating $90 rolls of sushi next to Aaron Eckhart. NYC wins again. (and expense accounts)

69 > Now I need to buy a new cell phone so I can keep up with Twitter?

You know, I got a really awesome, cute Chocolate LG for Christmas last year. Totally stylish and I love it, but it doesn't support any of the third-party applications to get Twitter on my phone. So I had to get *another* phone just to support this stupid web service. You'd think Twitter would be equal opportunity. I mean, even people who can't afford multiple phones like to read about soup!

Chapter 4

Work It, Twits

70 > Your boss wants you *on* Twitter

Bosses of the world are getting all hot and bothered over Twitter, and, I'm sorry to say, it's even worse if your boss is a woman over forty. Why? I got one word for you: Oprah. So now, no matter what you do for work, be it telesales or cleaning the local elementary school, your boss wants you to Twitter about it. It's what everyone is doing, whether it makes sense or not. No worries, boss. The economy is down, business is in the crapper, half of our work force got laid off, and tweeting has no relevance to what I do. It's cool though. Oprah said it was a good idea, and I do whatever Oprah tells me to do.

TWIT STAT

Twitter.com is a top-fifty site that reaches more than 23 million U.S. people monthly. The site attracts a young adult, slightly more female than male audience. The typical visitor reads Perez Hilton and subscribes to *Entertainment Weekly*.

71 > Your boss wants you *off* Twitter

And now we have a conundrum because as soon as you get on Twitter, your boss wants you off. Why? The economy is down, business is in the crapper, half of our work force got laid off, and tweeting has no relevance to what you do. Wait. Didn't I just say that?

72 > You got turned down for a job because you don't tweet

Dear potential employers: You know what I do during the workday? I tend to do my job. Yeah, I tend to work. Sometimes I'll get up to get some coffee, and on occasion I'll write a friend a quick e-mail regarding evening plans, but, by and large, I do actual work during the workday. That means I have little time for tweeting. That's why I find it so flabbergasting to hear that I am less attractive as a potential employee because I'm not an avid Twit. Here's a little bit of advice: the more you make people hang out on Twitter, Facebook, and other social networking sites, the less time they spend doing their actual jobs.

fail wail

██████: Fail whale says no profile image updates today . . .

73 > Twitter makes no sense without a TweetDeck, but your boss makes you Twitter anyway

And there we have it. Talking into a vacuum. The absolute worse part about Twitter is social-networking-ignorant bosses who insist you get on your freaking "Twitter blog" (yes, I realize that Twitter is not a blog, but try telling her that) and track the progress. As I've said a million times before, no one seems to understand what Twitter is and what the benefits of using it are. I'm sure it works great for marketing professionals, but we don't all work in publicity or marketing. This is bandwagon mentality and we all have Oprah and Ashton to blame for it. I know I'm going to burn in hell for this, but I'm turning on you, Oprah.

Insipid Status Update

@▒▒▒▒▒▒▒▒: I love that my dream inspires people around the world. It is amazing and I feel blessed every day that I have the ability to give so much.

74 > And now I'm freaking hooked!

Twitter has become like a brain-splicing drug. I feel like Bob Arctor in *A Scanner Darkly*; thanks to work forcing me onto Twitter, it has become my substance D. Twitter is completely useless, but then you get to a point where you're all like, "OMG! I can follow Ozzy Osbourne's every thought. How profound!" The downside: Ozzy doesn't make any more sense on Twitter than he does in real life.

75 > And now you're supposed to join a group?

Only, on Twitter they call them "Twibes." As my friend Amy says, "What's a Twibe? A collective of baby cavemen? Seems the most logical answer to me. And what does one do in a Twibe? Bang out virtual "dwums"?

76 > Your boss keeps calling it Twister, but still insists on you improving the social networking imprint of your company

During my last annual review one of my goals—my written goals—was to improve my department's social networking imprint through the use of Twister. Twister? Of course, he meant Twitter, but bosses are so scared of falling behind when it comes to adopting "the next hot thing" evidently they don't even have time to figure out what it's called, or what the real benefit of using it might be. So we're stuck juggling a million social networking trends without any real regard for whether they're actually going to help our company or not. And people wonder why we spend so much time surfing the Net during the workday. . . .

77 > Nowhere to hide

Facebook allows you to block your boss, your ex, your mom, or anyone else you never want to find you. Twitter doesn't offer the same sort of privacy measures. Finding someone on Twitter is easier than finding lice on a monkey. A quickie name search and suddenly you're flapping in the wind, free for all to see. Everyone can find you on Twitter, and they often do. Even the skanky guy who you totally shouldn't have given your business card to Friday night.

78 > Twitter judgment

The only way to keep any semblance of privacy on Twitter is by locking your tweets and making them private. The problem here is when you run into real, live Twats—Twitterers who pass judgment toward your interest in privacy. You know, like the passive aggressive guy over the cubicle wall who listens in on your phone conversations. Don't take it too hard, though. This is microblogging, so he's only passing microjudgment.

79 > The Twitter haunt

That person who makes you sponsor every freaking thing her kid does just found you on Twitter. Now you don't just have to pretend not to see her kid's sponsorship sign-up sheet every time you want a candy bar in the break room, you also have to pretend not to see it every time you log in to Twitter. Twitter is a fundraising mom's best friend. How else can you barrage a list of hundreds of people with pleas to help your kid get that free trip to Florida by purchasing a $20 canister of stale popcorn? No one is going to call you twelve times a day to ask you to do that, but they sure as heck will tweet you into a bloody pulp.

80 > Your cubemate just Twittered you

Dude! Come on! You are in the next freaking cube. The saying "What brings us together is sure to tear us apart" sure holds true here. I'm not even asking you to get up from your desk, just turn your stinkin' head. Once upon a time, it was considered bad social etiquette to talk to someone without making eye contact. Now it's somehow okay to talk to them without even turning around, or opening your mouth. I guess progress—and "creativity"—allows us to be socially impotent a-holes.

81 > Corporate Twits

I don't understand some of these corporate Twitter accounts. Virgin America, for example. I guess it would make sense if they'd alert us all to some upcoming deals or offers, but that's not what they do. What they do is chitchat with SeattleBiker and try to woo Rainn Wilson to "jump on board" again. Actually, I feel kind of bad for VA. Rainn doesn't seem interested, and that makes VA look like the kid with headgear at a high school dance.

82 > I avoid the Net so I can get work done, and still I Twitter

Somehow, Twittering has become workplace acceptable. It becomes okay to Twitter between tasks and to receive a tweet on your Crackberry in meetings. Well, maybe it's not okay, but it sure is easy to hide or pass off as actual work. The problem here is, Twitter follows you wherever you go. Even if you decide to avoid the Interwebs so you can focus on a task at hand, you can still receive a tweet to your phone. And that makes you want to tweet back. And that turns you into a total a-hole who tweets 24/7, even when you're having lunch with your ninety-two-year-old grandfather who doesn't understand Twitter. And when you try to tell him what you're doing he frowns and says, "Well, that just sounds dirty . . . are you on drugs?" True story. Turn the hearing aid on, Grandpa.

Chapter 5

Twitterrific!
Code Words and Apps Galore

83 > Attack of the @?

I'm sorry, but isn't @ an e-mail thing? I don't know. I just don't like seeing it on Twitter. It just reminds me of how I used to e-mail people once upon a time. How at one time, communication between two people was to be enjoyed privately and you didn't need to craft a reply witty enough to impress them—as well as the hundreds of other acquaintances following along. And to think I used to bemoan the death of the handwritten letter. Who would have thought it possible for things to get worse? I mean, at least with e-mail people could insert cute little emoticons that made you feel special. Now everyone talks like those robots from the original *Battlestar Galactica*.

Insipid (Celeb) Status Update

@JessicaSimpson: The best part about fame is the swag...OMG

84 > Hashing the hell out of things

Dude, I know you're trying to create a buzz and I know you're trying to collect followers (we ALL know you're trying to create followers), but when you continually hash the hell out of your posts, it doesn't look like you're writing on trended topics, it looks like your cat sat on your keyboard and then hit "update." Just choose wisely, man, that's all I ask. Don't be a hash-hole.

Insipid (Celeb) Status Update

> **MissKellyO (Kelly Osbourne):** working on mum's twitter she doesn't think it would be fare to do because she would have to have someone else do it for her! fingers crossed

85 > Excessive RT is bad, but an occasional RT is necessary

True, I hate it when people over-RT (retweet), but sometimes you really want to forward on some good information—like when Debbie Gibson talks about *Mega Shark vs. Giant Squid*. That is a movie no one wants to miss, so it's important to RT—without a second to spare (no, I'm serious). This is why I find it so befuddling that there is no RT button on tweets. I can reply or I can favorite, but I can't RT. And that, once again, causes me to wonder if the founders of Twitter even use their stupid product.

Twit Lingo

Twiccups (noun): When Twitter is having hiccups.

---

86 > Attack of the TwitBots!

One of the big problems with Twitter are the robot followers or followers who simply follow everyone—but they do so at a price. And they do it without souls. These TwitBots will request to follow you, but they are a vengeful species and, should the time come when you choose to unfollow them, they have software that will automatically unfollow you right back. They're all about the symbiosis of Twitter. Don't be fooled into thinking they give a shit about your soup.

87 > FoodFeed:
Taking your eating disorder to the Twittosphere

FoodFeed allows you to share what you eat with everyone, from anywhere. First, you add @having as a friend on Twitter and then post your food updates, such as @having a BLT. Your meal selection will be fed to your Twitter followers for all to see and judge you by. That way, when you start to feel fat, you have hundreds of people who can say #IToldYouSo! And you thought it took a complex psychological makeup to cause an eating disorder. But Twitter has simplified things and now you too can have anorexia in 140 characters or fewer!

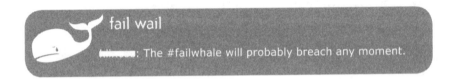

fail wail

████████: The #failwhale will probably breach any moment.

88 > Measuring my "Twinfluence"

As if Twitter wasn't out to make me feel insecure enough, first by telling me I talk too much (i.e. use too many characters), now it wants me to know just what tiny influence I have in the world with sites like Twinfluence, which give even the most latent tweeters a ranking. That's right, let's turn this into a popularity contest. And let's remind the little people how little they actually are. It's cool, though—the world needs ants. Without ants, soil would be crap and the world would wither and die. I'm here to dig through your soil Barack and Oprah; just let the ants do the toiling while you both look nice and pretty.

Chapter 6

Retweeting, Trolling, and Shameless Plugging

89 > You call it viral; we call it annoying

When you open a Twitter account to comment on your own Twitter account, you're not fooling anyone. No, seriously, we all know what you're doing. Sure, I'm down with you having a work account and a private account—I can even see the benefits—but don't think you have us fooled. What you're doing is just plain tacky.

90 > Do not feed the trolls

"Crack whore" is typically a name I only let close family members call me, but somehow . . . let's call him FakeDave . . . FakeDave found out the way to get right to my heart. I also really liked when he brought up my favorite pastime by posting an @reply to me about lesbian porn. FakeDave knows the way to a woman's heart. Sadly, the higher your profile on Twitter, the more susceptible you are to trolls. But as long as they know your family's pet name for you, like FakeDave did for me, all should be forgiven.

91 > TwitFights!

It does get a little funny when people fight publicly on Twitter. Nothing says schoolyard fun like a barrage of @replies, publicly dressing down one of the folks you follow. Get a room, people.

Insipid Status Update

@██████: hey, i still have the # for twitter on my cell phone. whatever. im bored

92 > Moon over My-spammy

There is nothing I hate more than when you follow someone and the first contact you get from them is a tweet or a direct message that says, "Thanks for following me! To earn extra money in your spare time, click here!" If I want to earn extra money I'll meet you in a back alley, just like I do with everyone else. Don't broadcast my side job to the whole world.

93 > Take it to your blog

It just goes to show, given the opportunity people will TALK ABOUT THEIR CATS. Isn't that what your blog is for? Isn't that the most appropriate place to talk about "Fluffer's" exploits around the sandbox and beyond? Fourteen tweets a day—every day—about how much you love that darn thing is a great big, flashing, neon sign that you've progressed far beyond microblogging. It's time to just call it what it is: blogging. So why don't you get off of Twitter and start yourself a blog? Consider it a promotion.

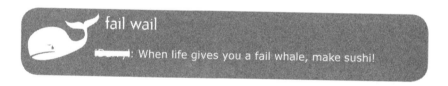

fail wail

When life gives you a fail whale, make sushi!

94 > Follow Fridays

I'm sure this started out as a good idea, but it has rapidly gone downhill because people are so bloody indiscriminate. Follow Fridays are meant to promote cool things that a fellow tweeter is doing, but most people recommend with such reckless abandon that their tweets look more like daisy chains: @follow1 @follow2 @follow3 @follow4 @follow5 #FollowFriday. Why the hell would I click on any of their names? A little info, folks? Could I get some? Just a little info about why I want to follow someone would be nice.

95 > Music Mondays

Want to know the best way to learn about crappy Top 40 music that you can hear on any mainstream radio station? Music Mondays! It would be one thing if anyone posted anything new, but I really don't need to turn to Twitter to learn about Beyoncé. No hate on Beyoncé, believe me, no hate at all, but I think I *may* have heard her music before.

....

Twit Lingo

Twitch (verb): Getting the urge to tweet. Also one of the first symptoms of tweetaholism.

....

96 > Linkless posting

But if you do post something remotely interesting, could you please post a link? Just shouting out what you like doesn't help anyone out. This is the world wide web. And that means interactivity. Did you forget what that was all about while you were busy tweeting off?

97 > Other people's tweets

As if tweeting into a vacuum wasn't hard enough. Now we have people who don't even really tweet at all. All they do is post what other people tweet. This is what we call "excessive retweeting." It's when people have absolutely nothing of interest to say at any time, so they just retweet the people they follow. Problem is, many times you follow your friends, and you happen to share other friends with them. Which means you're seeing the hysterical tweet by LizPW not only the first time when she posted it two hours ago, but fifty more times by all your mutual friends. You know what, folks? If I want constant repetition I'll get myself a freaking parrot. Or I'll become a Buddhist and take up chanting and shit.

TWIT STAT

The use of Twitter is highly intertwined with the use of other social media; both blogging and social network use increase the likelihood that an individual also uses Twitter. Twitter users and status updaters are also a mobile bunch; as a group they are much more likely to be using wireless technologies—laptops, handhelds, and cell phones—for Internet access, or cell phones for text messaging.

Chapter 7

Celeb Twittergasm: The Big O Has Joined the 21st Century

98 > Oprah, there's really NO NEED TO SHOUT!!

Oprah seems really nice and all, but that lady loves to write in caps. And sometimes she even writes IN ALL CAPS. For example, her first Twitter post was one of those SHOUT FROM THE HIGHEST MOUNTAIN kind of posts. She's so enthusiastic and when I watch her on TV it gets me all fired up for feeling positive and empowered and stuff—and then I start thinking about buying my neighbor a car—but on Twitter it's a little daunting. I'm just trying to figure out if she's yelling at me or with me. Because when Oprah yells *at* you I think it must mean you're fighting an upward battle in life and no one is ever going to love you.

Twit Lingo

Twitetiquette (noun): How to behave on Twitter.

99 > "HI Yall! Brit Brit here, just wanted to update you on the size of my vagina. . . ."

Okay, that totally sucked. First of all, I had nightmares for weeks about a vagina with teeth chasing me down Mulholland Drive batting at me with a huge green umbrella. It was terrifying. It was like *20,000 Leagues Under the Sea* meets *Xanadu* meets *Baywatch* meets *Troop Beverly Hills* meets *L.A. Confidential*. Anyway, if someone as upstanding, classy, and decent as Britney gets her account hacked, what does that mean for the rest of us? We're all susceptible and the Huge Va-Jay-Jay Hacker of 2009 can strike any of us at any time! No one is safe and I don't think Twitter gives a shit.

Twit Lingo

Twitcidents (noun): Twitter-related incidents or accidents. *(Happens a lot to Dutch Twitterers who tweet while on their bikes, in twaffic.)*

---

100 > Democratization of media, my ass, Ashton! This just strokes your insatiable ego

Right on, Ashton. You broke a million and still we can't stop you. You're faster than a freaking speeding bullet and able to leap tall buildings in a single bound and all that awesome stuff that makes you a superhero. You hear that? It's me applauding you. I hope that makes you feel popular. No single person has ever reached 1 million followers before. Wouldn't it be hilarious if we punk'd Ashton by UNfollowing him on the same day? I wonder if anyone has LOST 1 million followers in one day before? Now, that would be an impressive record! But would Ashton survive? Would Demi dump him? Inquiring minds want to know.

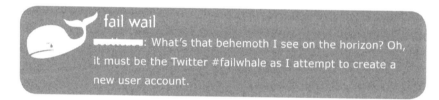

fail wail

███████: What's that behemoth I see on the horizon? Oh, it must be the Twitter #failwhale as I attempt to create a new user account.

101 > Demi—get an identity!

Really, Demi? Your username is "mrskutcher." I know you guys are trying to promote the romance in your relationship, but this just makes me want to gag. It's getting so you're hardly discernable from Katie Holmes. Demi, darling! Speak up! And all your posts are about your "hubby" or Susan Boyle. (BTW, if you're friends with Susan can you please ask her to do something about her eyebrows?)

102 > I've watched Paris Hilton have sex and she won't let me follow her?

Everyone on the planet has seen Paris Hilton have sex in night vision, and yet she's got her freaking Twitter account in lockdown. Pardon me, but there really isn't anything more ridiculous. You actually have to ask her permission to follow her. Can you say control freak? What is the criteria to follow Paris Hilton? Is this like some sort of sorority rush? Or maybe Tinkerbell makes the final decision on who makes the cut. . . .

103 > Okay, Paris finally let me follow her and now she's spamming me about *Dancing with the Stars*

So I had to wait a week (with bated breath, I must add) for Paris Hilton to allow me to follow her and now I get no action. Where's Doug Reinhardt when we need him? For chrissake, Paris, you have a captive audience of more than 150,000 followers. Do you think you could give us a little more info than where you get your highlights done? And, for real, the *Dancing with the Stars* updates are getting really old. Tell the truth, did you have a financial stake in that show, because the updates are out of hand.

104 > Ryan Seacrest posts like a soccer mom

Okay, Ryan. We know you're as wholesome as apple pie—you don't have to cram it down our throats with your tweets. I can almost see you smiling at us with your bland good looks as you give us your dull updates on the coffee in the break room and how much you love *The Hills*. This is not the "need to know" info I was hoping for, Ryan. I mean, the world is dying to know what makes Ryan Seacrest tick and this is the drivel that we get? Well, it's back to the tabloids for me, my friend. You had your chance, but I need a more reliable source that doesn't bore me to tears, so I'll follow TMZ, thank you very much.

(CELEB)

Insipid ^Status Update

> **MissKellyO (Kelly Osbourne):** just so you know shunt means Shitty c**t!

105 > Ashlee Simpson Wentz takes sibling rivalry to dazzling new heights

If there was any doubt that Ashlee Simpson feels inferior to Jessica, that doubt will be laid to rest when you read her Twitter feed. Yes, Ashlee, we know you're a blissful newlywed with your incessant updates about how wonderful your hubby is. Way to rub it in to your thousands of followers and mom-jeans-wearing older sister. But who needs a reality show like *Newlyweds* when you tweet about your every forced and nauseating swoon?

106 > Elisabeth Hasselbeck's scary "view"

Further evidence that Elisabeth Hasselbeck is a right-wing freakazoid who wants to eat your soul and then regurgitate it to feed to the Satan babies she's had with George W. Bush. Now we get minute-by-minute updates on her Susie Sunshine conservatism.

107 > Nicole Ritchie disses after-dinner hugs

Nicole Ritchie is anti-hugs! And anti-grammar! She totally posted that she doesn't want to hug people when she leaves dinner parties. Nicole, but if anyone should be worried about getting cooties it's the people you hug, and not the other way around. You just kind of look a little skanky, that's all I'm sayin'. I'm just trying to help.

108 > Even on Twitter Martha Stewart talks down to me

I know you're perfect, Martha. We all know you're perfect. And I know you can whip up a gorgonzola and spinach truffle risotto with a port wine reduction while arranging a bouquet of peonies and posting a status update with your perfectly pedicured toes. I know you think you're better than me, and I thank God for Twitter so I can hear how much I suck on an hourly basis. My therapist loves it too.

....

Twit Lingo

TweetUp (verb): When Twitterers meet in person.

....

109 > Poor Richard Simmons only has 891 followers

I'm following Richard Simmons, but only because I'm a fan of the under-dog. The poor guy with his enthusiastic disco Afro only has 891 followers at my last count. With the age demographic that's on Twitter, you'd think he'd be a superstar in the Twittosphere—or you'd think he'd at least measure up to Bruce Jenner. But maybe Richard's fans are too busy sweatin' to the oldies to tweet. Maybe Richard needs to marry a bitchy socialite like Kris Kardashian Jenner who pits her children against one another to get some street cred. But who is a bitchy gay socialite? Maybe Carson Kressley? He's pretty.

110 > Tea Time with Neil Gaiman

Neil, I love you, but stop retweeting people "drinking tea". In most cases, bestselling author Gaiman is a model Twit. A seasoned blogger since 2001, he knows how to keep things short, sweet, and informative. But everyone has their Achilles' heel and, for Gaiman, it seems to be tea. Darling Neil, we know you're British and we know how much you Brits love your tea, m'kay. You don't have to pour it down our throats.

111 > Shaquille O'Neal—bringin' it to the people

The Shaq took back his identity by opening his own Twitter account, after an authentic-sounding imposter entertained thousands of fans in his name with a pretty spot-on impression. But you know, I kinda miss the imposter Shaq. At least the guy impersonating Shaquille O'Neal actually came up with witty quips to entertain followers. The real Shaquille seems to use his account for @ attacks, with no real updates to speak of. It's like being at a cocktail party where you can only hear one side of the conversation. No fun at all.

112 > William Shatner is a pimp

And I don't mean that in a good way. I don't mean he's a big pimpin' daddy—I mean he uses his Twitter account for little more than pimping his celebrity. We all try to tell ourselves that William Shatner isn't shallow—that the Captain Kirk and Denny Crane characters are only characters. Eh, we're lying to ourselves. Why can't he be more like LeVar Burton and actually connect with his followers? Kirk, why can't you be more like Geordie?

113 > Dr. Phil only follows one person

What's up with that, Doc? I think this pretty much backs up the assumptions everyone has about you being a self-righteous jerk. You really don't care what anyone—anyone—else has to say? Well, this speaks volumes. *This* is why your advice never makes any goddamn sense. Maybe if you listened to something else besides the sound of your own mellifluous voice, people would know what the heck you were talking about once in a while. Christ, Phil—you're not even following Oprah, and she freaking MADE YOU. Talk about a lack of gratitude.

Twit Lingo

Tweet In (noun): When Twitterers get together at an agreed time to Twitter.

---

114 > Olivia Munn doesn't need to tell us every time she's shooting

Olivia—you host *Attack of the Show*! It's your full-time job. That means you're supposed to be up on all things geek-related. You'd think you'd know how to craft an interesting tweet. But all you talk about is filming and pie. And pie. And pie. Just freaking eat the pie, Olivia! I'm sick of hearing about it.

(CELEB)

Insipid ^Status Update

MrsSOsbourne (Sharon Osbourne): i am happy to be apart of the twitter world all followers welcome!

115 > Just 'cause they let you follow them doesn't mean they'll be your friend

The most disappointing thing about celebrity tweeters is the slap in the face of reality you get when you follow them. It feels like instant connection, but it's not. You'll frequently get updates from their assistant or publicist, or you'll get obligatory updates that give you no insight into anything, no more than an article in *Star* magazine would give you. And they certainly aren't going to follow you back. So your grand notion of being invited to all these glamorous Hollywood parties because Ashton Kutcher and Demi Moore happen to find your tweets hilarious? It ain't gonna happen. They're going to use you to up their Twitter rankings and ignore you when they've got their fill. Welcome to Hollywood.

Chapter 8

Not So Tweet: Beware of Bird Shit

116 > Fun with redirects!

Oh no, I am NOT falling for that TinyURL you have there. No bloody way. A blind URL is a dangerous URL; there's porn lurking in that sneaky little shortcut tweet. How the hell do I know what you have hiding in there? I am not going to click it. Especially since my boss is making me tweet while at work. Last thing I need is to click on a TinyURL to read about *Drag Me to Hell* and end up watching a clip from *Girls Gone Wild Extreme*.

117 > Cheap online imposters and attack of the clones

As if Twitter weren't annoying enough, now we have a whole litany of imposter sites out there. Plurk, Zannel, Kwippy, Presently—they all saw what was arguably a good thing and decided to jump right on board. If imitation is the highest form of flattery, well, then Twitter has positively reached icon status.

How can I annoy thee? Let me count the ways. Right now I only see a handful, but I'm sure more are to follow.

118 > Why isn't there a better way to see who I'm following?

Correct me if I'm wrong, but it does seem like half the point of Twitter is to follow people, right? I mean, they call us followers, so one would assume following is the whole point. So why is it there is no real way to see who you're following on the Twitter site? If I want to see what my friend Amy is up to, I'm totally screwed. Why? Because Amy had to get all creative with her name and I can never remember what it is. So I have to send Amy an e-mail and ask her what her Twitter name is again so I can connect with—oh, right—NetEditrix. This might cause one to ask why, if I'm e-mailing Amy, I don't just start a conversation with her over e-mail. Good question.

119 > The more you tweet the less you know

There is something very profound about the whole Twitter experience. It seems almost like a parable for life: The more you follow the less you know. That's because (a) you can't easily find your friends (as I just said) and (b) the more people you follow the less likely you are to pick up on a tweet by someone you actually care about. I do care about Jimmy Fallon, but he is hardly my best friend, and—let's be honest—the guy tweets a lot. I really would rather know what my childhood friend who moved to Tahiti is doing.

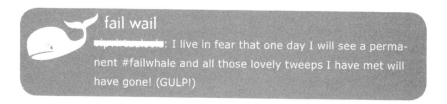

fail wail

██████████: I live in fear that one day I will see a permanent #failwhale and all those lovely tweeps I have met will have gone! (GULP!)

120 > Taking geekdom to a whole new level

We now have Twitter role-playing—a whole new venue for geeks to get their jollies and pretend they're someone else. Some interesting ones are characters from *Deadwood*, *Harry Potter*, and *Doctor Who*. I'm sure there are even Civil War re-enactments on Twitter, I've just yet to find them. So, as though role-playing wasn't a geeky enough activity, now the social misfits need to one up themselves by containing their geekdom in 140-character clips. It seems like the geeks are taking over the earth even when they're busy pretending they're someone they're not. How do they have time to procreate?

121 > Twitter fakers

Egads! All this time I thought I was following Tina Fey and I was all, "Wow, in real life Tina Fey isn't even that funny. I'm way funnier than she is. I'm totally going to try out for SNL!" But then, come to find out, I was following a faker! A total Fey faker! And you know, it's as easy as pie for someone to sign up for Twitter and pretend they're someone they're not. Like, I absolutely thought Britney Spears and I were becoming fast friends and I was pretty psyched when she invited me out for lunch during my last visit to L.A. Imagine my surprise when I finally met her and she was a 300-pound Latino man named Brian. Trust no one, people. Not even Britney.

Insipid Status Update

@j███████████: I go to stores in pjs and wear my oversized glasses inside; I don't want the paparazzi taking pictures.

122 > Username squatting

It's not just for URLs anymore. Whenever there is money to be made, you can be certain some a-hole will do his best to destroy your faith in humanity. And that's exactly what's happening with Twitter usernames. And it's getting some people's panties in a serious bunch. Come on people. Can't we all just get along? It shouldn't matter what our usernames are, we're all Twits on the inside.

Twit Lingo
Tweet-dropping (verb): Eavesdropping on Tweeps. Also known as lurking.

> **@JessicaSimpson:** Just overcame my fear of sharks by kissing a killer whale

123 > Beware of the bunnies!

Between the tweeting chicks and the bastard bunnies, Twitter is like some Easter prank gone terribly wrong. Last year's security breach when the "pretty bunny" nearly took down tweeters by the thousand was a tough blow to the land of twee. Promises of some adult YouTube video action took Twits into the depths of virus hell, transforming your Twittering machine into a lethargic node, good for nothing but a trip to the IT guy. You would think with the promise of bunnies and adult videos it would have resulted in a totally awesome day. But those bastards took away all that is joyous about bunnies and porn. Is nothing sacred?

PART 2

FACEBOOK: A FACE ONLY A MOTHER COULD LOVE

The Internet is just a world passing around notes in a classroom.

—Jon Stewart

Chapter 9

The Great Facebook Debate

124 > If it ain't broke, don't fix it

Who is Facebook getting all of the ideas for "improvements" from? It sure as hell isn't its users. Do you ever get the feeling that all the user-interface designers camp out in the fancy Facebook break room in Palo Alto, eating "special" brownies, talking about ways they can mess with its users? As soon as we get comfortable with one change (and all of those user groups that are against the "new format" have finally simmered down), Facebook, like clockwork, announces a new layout that's going to be completely different than the last, making you feel like a blind housekeeper came in and rearranged your room.

125 > Showing your privates

Feeling a little exposed? That's because Facebook has decided to make all of our status updates and wall postings public by default—with nary a peep of an announcement. So the next time Facebook asks "What's on your mind?" I'm going to say, "Janelle thinks Facebook is a total lying, two-timing a-hole!" When you change the rules you gotta tell the players, FB. What you did sits about as well as week-old Indian food followed by a Pop Rocks and Tabasco chaser.

126 > Bitch and moan en masse

But as much as it annoys me that Facebook keeps changing stuff, it annoys me more how vehemently angry some users get about the format change. Must we remind you that Facebook is free? And all that photo and video storage doesn't come cheap. Remember when you lived at your parents' house and complained about how life just wasn't fair because they got to call the shots? And then you found out not only was life fair, but it was a helluva lot simpler before you needed to figure out how to pay for everything? That's what's going on now, my friend. So shut your trap before Mom makes us pay to hang out in her basement.

facebook FACT Facebook was originally called "Facemash."

127 > When Facebook became a Twit

Color me confused. What website am I on? I'd swear to God I logged in to Facebook, but it's starting to look more and more like Twitter every time I blink. Now Facebook, don't you go and start getting all "MySpace" on us by copying the latest flavor of the month. It takes a strong person (or strong social networking site, as it were) to know who they are. Don't cave in and become something you're not just because the new kid in town is seemingly more popular. That'll just make you look desperate.

facebook FACT

Facebook founder and owner Mark Zuckerberg was inspired by a site called Hot Or Not, the granddaddy of wasting time online. At hotornot. com, people submit photos of themselves, and users rate them on a scale from one to ten. Good times, indeed!

128 > Death to blogs

And again, I really don't know what's what. Will Facebook be the undoing of the personal blog? Now I'm not a huge fan of the self-absorbed personal blog. I have no desire to read about some vanilla thirty-something who takes pictures of herself drunk and her cat looking bored, but at least with blogs there was room for true self-expression. At least the blogger could exercise some creative control over her content. It's like Facebook has put all the bloggers into parochial school uniforms and forced them to stand in single file while the nuns crack their knuckles every time they write with their left hands. And that, my friends, kinda makes me want to blog.

Allison is so happy to be home after a long day at work.
1 minute ago · Comment · Like

---

129 > When Facebook makes you an essayist

This totally stresses me out. All I want to do is post a teeny, pithy status update, but then I realize that my mom is going to read this, as well as the cute and witty wordsmith I have a crush on, as well as the ex who I know finds subtext in the word "and." Instead of being smart and staying the hell off Facebook, I log in to the damn thing and find a snarky response to a status update, which makes me feel like I have to explain myself. Forty-five minutes later I've posted an epic novel longer and more convoluted than *Gravity's Rainbow* in a vain effort to explain myself. Facebook has taken self-absorption to the next level, and evidently I'm on the express elevator up.

130 > The condescending status update

I know you dared to follow your dream while I've been sitting rotting in a cubicle. And you know what? I'm really proud of you. I think it rules that you're recording with some unnamed flautist who worked with Billy Corgan, which has now made you Billy Corgan's best friend eleven times removed. And I know how "blessed" you think you are to be working with "such wildly talented people who believe in the music" you're making. You're living the dream. You're cooler than I am. We all know this. Please don't repost that sentiment every damn day. Thank you.

131 > Are they making us a social experiment?

Wait, why does Facebook keep changing stuff on me? It's gotten so frustrating that I wouldn't be the least bit surprised to find out that when I joined Facebook I somehow gave them the right to put a chip in my brain so they could monitor and amuse themselves over every temper tantrum I have. I keep getting invites to join "The Ultimate Social Experiment" group; I'm more than a little convinced that we, the users, are the ultimate social experiment, and Facebook has a pretty darn sick sense of humor.

facebook FACT
Facebook has never been a cash cow. In 2005 it lost $3.63 million. *(You gotta love that business model.)*

132 > Is this shit mine . . . or Property of Facebook?

Thank you, Facebook, for giving me back my photos, but you've totally lost my trust. Once you lie to me, you can't go back. I didn't think it was very nice of you to clandestinely claim rights to all of my photos. What use you have for five dozen photos of me with my eyes closed, sporting a double chin, is beyond me. The point is, you wanted to have your cake and eat it too, and that's just wrong. You wanted the "just in case" option to be all yours. Well, that's pretty greedy, Facebook. And nobody likes a pig.

133 > The lazy Like button

All right, I'll admit it. I'm as guilty of hitting the Like button as much as anyone. During those times when you need your Facebook fix, but are too tuckered to say anything of substance, the Like button is an invaluable tool. But there are those who overdo it. Like drinking beer, you have to know when you're taking it too far and when you need to just call it a night. I know it's tempting because it seems so easy, but it makes you look disinterested, noncommittal, or just really lazy. Resist the urge.

facebook FACT

Using an automated script, two MIT students were able to download more than 70,000 Facebook profiles from four schools (MIT, NYU, the University of Oklahoma, and Harvard) as part of a research project on Facebook privacy published on December 14th, 2005.

134 > What if I Don't Like it? Where's the button for that?

There is some seriously offensive stuff on Facebook. Such as . . . photos of your brother's hairy nipple, or when your recent ex suddenly updates his status to "in a relationship," or when your college roommate starts posting status updates about poopy diapers, or when your cousin posts another Jonas Brothers video. No one should have to be subjected to such things, and a Do Not Like button would let people know that, in truth, it's really sad that you take more photos of your Porsche than most people take of their children, it's never going to love you back, and we don't want to see another damn picture of it.

Amber is sleeping.

5 minutes ago · Comment · Like

(Author note: No you're not. You're typing on your computer. Go to bed!)

facebook FACT Despite slow revenue streams, the company was valued at $8 billion in late 2006. This was extrapolated from potential future earnings.

135 > People who still put "is" in their status updates

Okay, they got rid of the "is" in the status update for a reason. The reason, if you didn't already guess, is that the "is" was too passive. Facebook finally straightened up and started getting active; how's about you start doing the same? Just let it go guys; living in the passive past will do you no good. It's time to step it up and stop taking a sledgehammer to grammar. There is no need to craft nonsensical sentences like, "Allison is coconut water." Instead, try something like, "Allison likes coconut water." Now isn't that liberating? (Forgive my use of the passive here.)

136 > People who only put "is" in their status updates, trying to be all existential or something

All right, Sartre, we all get it. Because we've all seen it a million times before. Your ego has fully transcended, you are infinite and overflowing and to ask you to reflect any more on what you are is fated to result in anxiety. No need to understand or describe, my friend. Just. Be. Yep, we're all "condemned to be free" even within the confines of a 420-character status update. Granted, the point of an existentialist status update is to remain misunderstood and, therefore "infinite," so I'll just pretend that I'm floating in your indefinable essence. Deal?

137 > Stop making me talk in the third person!

Facebook is such a control freak. I hate that they make us talk in the third person. Let's get real for a second. If I struck up a conversation with you in a bar and said, "Janelle is thirsty for a rum and Coke," you'd think I was an idiot, right? So why must Facebook make every one of us talk like we're suffering from dissociative disorder? People who refer to themselves in the third person are, in no uncertain terms, douchebags. Thank you, Facebook, for making sure I fall into that category. Because I was having a hard time getting there on my own.

138 > Social networking purgatory

You can run, but you can't ever, ever, EVER hide. Despite your best efforts to break free of the hold Facebook has on your life, you can never actually kill your account. Instead, when you think that the account you created is closed, it's really languishing in a sort of social networking purgatory, waiting for you to free it from the closed-account shackles. Facebook has a stronger hold on your past than any satanic cult you could ever conceive of. So that's right. Those photos of you in the interpretive, feminist dance troupe you uploaded in 2007 are still there, and seemingly *always* will be.

facebook FACT

There are more than 250 million active Facebook users worldwide.

139 > Mort à la resistance!

We can go on and on about how awful Facebook is, but the most frustrating thing about Facebook is those who don't join—or worse, those who have latent accounts. There are two factions in this world, those who Facebook and those who don't, and I'm afraid those who Facebook are winning. So, when it comes time for me to send out an invite to an event, there is nothing more frustrating than having to send it to the fifteen people who check their Facebook accounts and then two who don't. I'd like to say it's worth the extra effort to ensure that all are included, but the reality of the situation is, it's just a pain in the ass.

facebook FACT The Facebook Terms of Service are updated and revised almost monthly.

140 > Drunk Dialing 2.0

Ohhh . . . that was really embarrassing. And I let the whole world know about it. In Massachusetts all bars close at 1 A.M. That fact used to annoy me, but now I realize those blue laws were actually doing me a favor. If you're still drinking at 1 A.M., the possibility of embarrassment increases exponentially, so either go home or to a private party where only your closest friends will witness you trying to clean up an unexpected accident with your party dress. Why can't Facebook impose a blue law of some sort? Why can't they please "maintain" the site between the hours of 1 A.M. and 5 A.M.? Or take a cue from Google, who added the handy option of "Beer, er, Mail Goggles" to Gmail. It makes me think Facebook actually *enjoys* your drunken updates. If Facebook were a human it would totally be the friend who writes "sucker" on your forehead when you pass out.

141 > Facebook hates proofreaders

His Holiness the Dalai Lama has said, "There is no genuine second chance." And that sentiment is pretty dead on when it comes to Facebook. It's nothing short of humiliating when you post a status update with a glaring grammatical error so bad it makes you look like you dropped out of school in the eighth grade. Even worse is when all of your friends make fun comments that you don't want to delete. So you either remove a truly excellent conversation thread in order to hide your carelessness, or you keep the guffaw where you said you'd like to thank your mother "pubicly" for all her help moving this weekend. The choice is yours.

142 > When people become fans of "sleeping," yawning, etc.

For years I felt so alone. I actually lost sleep because I felt like a social outcast because of my unnatural affection for shuteye. I could go on for days about how much I love sleep and am so relieved that the day has come that I finally have 30,000 Internet friends with whom I can extol its virtues. What's even more awesome is that I can now see that twelve of my Facebook friends like sleep too! I don't know what the others are thinking; I may have to defriend some folks because I'm not into anyone who isn't into sleeping. Yeah, Sleeping rules. I'm so glad you think so too.

143 > Those "so and so must join Facebook" groups

Let's think about this for a minute: In order to actually see one of these groups, the person has to join Facebook. So all of your witty jabs and pleas for solidarity are wasted in the cybersphere as your friend who won't join Facebook is outside enjoying the sunshine and fresh air with his kid. So what is the purpose of these groups? Is it so we can all wallow in commiseration over the great gaping hole our friend's absence from Facebook has left on the world?

facebook FACT

Fearing that it may be used as a meeting point for dissidents, authorities in Iran and Syria have intermittently restricted access to Facebook.

144 > Killing e-mail softly

Facebook is a sneaky little bastard. I always thought it was weird that they not only didn't hotlink e-mail addresses in people's profiles, but they made e-mail addresses TIFFs that you can't even copy and paste. Little did I realize in my nascent days of Facebooking how insidious their plans were. Innocuous as it may seem, this annoyance is actually part of Facebook's scheming plan for world domination. A recent Nielsen study reported that more Internet users log in to check their Facebook profile than their e-mail.

That's right, Facebook has long planned to kill e-mail and only you can stop it. Get into the ring, folks, we're about to see an ultimate fighting match between Facebook and Gmail. I hope they wear those cool masks!

145 > If you're going to hijack e-mail, at least make it work!

If Facebook e-mail were a country, it would be communist Russia. You only have one option, you can't get out, and in that one option you can't even get the basic necessities. Like forwarding, or organizing, or HTML coding, or adding a new person to a thread: an average e-mailer's fundamental needs are not being met! I mean, sure, Facebook isn't killing any of its denizens (yet!), but they force you into using their backward application by making you unable to click on your contacts' e-mail addresses.

Kevin can't think of anything interesting to say.

17 minutes ago · Comment · Like

146 > You can spam me, but I can't send out a legitimate mass e-mail?

If you admit in one of your friend details that you don't really know the person, Facebook gets its panties all in a bunch. So you'd assume that it would be the idea to only be friends with people you know. And you'd assume that most people who accept your friend requests wouldn't mind hearing from you. So why is it that Facebook caps all group e-mails at twenty recipients? If I'm going home for the weekend, I have more friends and family than twenty that I'd like to meet up with. Thank you, Facebook, for making one more thing that's supposed to make my life easier a royal pain in the ass.

147 > You don't have to hit Reply All, people!

I don't even know where to aim my aggression with this one. But I think I'm going to blame it on the people who Reply All to threads. Especially when their response is "LOL!", ":-p", or "OMG!". We get a notification every time you do that and it drives me nuts. But maybe my aggression is misdirected. Maybe I should really be annoyed with Facebook for first hijacking e-mail and then all but making the Reply button undetectable. Hell, it's not a button at all—it's a discreet link. Facebook WANTS you to be an a-hole. And if you're not already, they will show you how.

148 > Facebook profile-name vigilantes

What the hell? This is my freaking Facebook account; I'll change my name if I want to. Maybe I did change my name to Jack Kaufmann. What of it? And who is Facebook to judge whether that's a real name or not? I know some people with some really crappy names. Some people are given questionable names when they're born and others would like to exercise their God-given right to go by such questionable names in their online persona. Just be glad Frank Zappa is dead, Facebook, otherwise I'd have to ask him to open a can of whoop ass on you.

149 > As soon as Facebook sucks you in, it shuts down for maintenance

Why is it that every third day some part of Facebook seems to be down for maintenance? As soon as I get sucked into the reality web series known as "My High School Friends," service goes down, people lose momentum, and the potential for carnage is dissipated beyond repair. This is worse than missing your favorite TV show. This is missing your favorite TV show and then when you tune in again they've decided to inexplicably drop the story line and start on a new one. And there's no option for TiVo.

150 > Rolls out new design and leaves me behind

What was the logic behind rolling out the latest Facebook upgrade? Because I was the last of all my friends privy to the big reveal. And I call bullshit. I was the first of my friends to join Facebook in March 2007 but the last to see the upgrade? That just doesn't seem fair. It actually seems like I'm being punished for my loyalty. Facebook, ever hear of the saying "make new friends but keep the old?" You got a great big stack o' gold here that's feeling a wee bit shafted.

151 > No search function for your Wall or status updates

So say someone posts something particularly awesome on your Wall or in response to your status updates. Let's just say it's about some really rad toothpaste. So you're about to go out and buy some new toothpaste and you're all, "Oh! Sara told me about this awesome toothpaste a few months ago." So you go on Facebook and then you find yourself paging through two months' worth of comments and links and status updates to find a stinkin' toothpaste referral. And then you've lost an hour of your life and end up using baking soda.

152 > They hold your videos hostage

Don't think for a second that you can share that video. Once it's on Facebook it's there to stay and there ain't no sharing that can take place. No way, no how you're downloading that thing. My parents are grandparents and their parents are still alive and when my grandparents see Facebook, steam starts pouring out of their ears and they start hitting the computer like a band of uncaged monkeys. Cut 'em some slack. All they want to do is see their granddaughter and share the video of her with every friend, family member, and friendly enough passerby. Facebook, if we download a video you won't lose all that's precious to you. This is called sharing; didn't your mother ever teach you to share?

153 > Hijackers *really* suck

People who don't comment on something you posted but then they post it on their own freaking Wall are a-holes. I have nothing more to say. Oh, except that they suck and they lack originality. At least "Like" it or something. I mean, make a little effort before stealing my idea!

154 > Direct URL swooners

You'd think they'd discovered a cure for cancer, the way people swooned over the Direct URL feature on Facebook. Within three minutes 200,000 had rushed the site and signed up. Of course, one of them was named Janelle. You know, I spend my whole darn life being the kid who couldn't have the cool mass-produced keychain with my name on it, and now some tech-geek has to steal my name. WTF?

155 > Out of sight doesn't mean out of mind anymore

You can "hide" the hell out of someone's status updates, but if they write on a friend's Wall or if they get tagged in another friend's photos, you're still going to see what they're up to, and that sucks. It takes a strong person to be able to always have someone in their periphery while never actually looking at them. A Zen person, actually. If you don't want to see the photos of your ex-roommate who duped you out of last month's rent so she could spend her summer in Iceland, the only real course of action you have is to block the bitch (not that I'm talking about anyone in particular. I'm not.).

156 > Now I've turned into one of those a-holes who updates from her phone

Everybody else is doing it! Remember the days when something awesome happened and you got so excited to go home and tell your friends about it. Or, even better, when your friends said something like, "Let's go out for drinks when you get back. I want to hear all about your trip!" No more. Now we've got the insta-updates. And, thanks to your obsession with updating from your phone, I really don't feel like I need to waste my time with you anymore. I'm sure you feel the same. Now I can get back to doing what's really important. Like playing Halo 2.

facebook FACT

Adding your mobile phone number to your Facebook profile increases the risk of mobile spamming.

157 > The FB hold

It really does get a hold on you. I've tried to close my account, just to take a little break and see if I miss it, but I can't bring myself to do so. Every time I log in with a plan to close it, someone posts something hilarious that I'd probably die or something if I never saw. Like, my leg would have fallen off if I didn't see all those YouTube videos of Susan Boyle. You know the feeling, right?

facebook FACT

Initially, Facebook membership was confined to Harvard students. Within a month, half the student body had signed up.

158 > Feeling fat when no one is looking

You know what rules? Logging in to my Facebook account on Sunday morning and seeing a stream of updates from all my friends who just got back from running their half-marathons and training for their tenth triathlons, while I'm sitting here in my sweatpants, stuffing my face with my second glazed cinnamon roll and washing it down with my whole milk latte. Don't trip on your next run. Wouldn't want you to sprain an ankle or anything.

159 > Facebook porn cops

At what point did Facebook become a convent? They now have a team of "porn cops" charged with what they claim is "enforcing decorum." It's all about the advertisers and it's kind of ridiculous. Especially when you think of what kind of dollars they could get if they started advertising for condoms, or lingerie, or something that makes their users feel sexy. As opposed to continually advertising for "weight loss secrets" for women thirty-two to forty-five. And what qualifies someone to be a porn cop anyway? How do you apply? 'Cause I think I'd be perfect.

160 > Facebook thinks I'm old and fat

And on that note. What makes Facebook think that when I'm looking at my exes frolicking with their children on the beach I want to hear I'm considered old and fat by advertisers? I don't want to see ads telling me how to banish my wrinkles just like Jennifer Aniston and how to whiten my teeth. You know what happens when people tell me that stuff in real life? I stop being friends with them.

facebook FACT

In 2004, The Facebook, now a company, registered the domain name Facebook.com—dropping "The" from its title.

Chapter 10

To Friend or Not to Friend (Unfortunately, That Is the Question)

161 > Strangers in the night, or "Who the hell is this person?"

Wait. Your name is Deiter Pop? Is that even a real name? And how do I know you when I've never even been to Berlin? I'm pretty sure I've never even seen you and since Facebook tells me we have no friends in common, I'm pretty sure you're mistaken. Unless you're using Facebook to make friends, in which case why don't you use that handy little feature called the messaging function to tell me why I should find you so fascinating. Because the photo of you standing there in front of . . . what is that? A Laundromat? Anyway your photo ain't convincing me.

162 > The leeches: The friends you can't get rid of

Hell hath no fury like a Facebooker scorned, it would seem. People can get pretty heated and vengeful when defriended. My advice to you is to defriend wisely. Because they come back. And, like adult acne, they will keep coming back unless you properly deal with them. And the only way to deal with them is to block them. For real. First send them an e-mail saying you're dead (if you can get a few friends to post condolence messages to your folks on your Wall, that helps maintain authenticity) and then block them. Make them think your bereaved family closed your account. It's the only way.

facebook FACT

West Wing creator Aaron Sorkin is developing a movie about Mark Zuckerberg and the origins of Facebook. *(What do you think they'll call it? West Face? Face West?)*

163 > The parasites:
The friends who steal all your friends

Hello? Was anyone planning on inviting me to this party? What is this crap? I log in one day and suddenly Jane Jones from college who went on to be a publicist (*big* surprise) is now friends with 80 percent of my Friend List. How did that happen? Oh, and now I'm seeing, horror of all horrors—she's sending out a bazillion mass e-mails to them. First of all, don't trust anyone who has more than 550 friends; that number is a pretty reliable rule of thumb. Second, you have every right to hop on a plane so you can personally bitch slap the friend who steals all your friends on Facebook and then proceeds to spam them.

Jennifer is training for her first 5k!
2 hours ago · Comment · Like

(Author note: I'm eating a cheese Danish.)

164 > Facebook etiquette:
What you don't know will get you defriended

It's hard enough letting real-life faux pas slide, but when friends post a series of angry and aggressive status updates that just reverberate on your screen for hours, until enough other friends push them down or you finally hide them from your feed, it's hard to let go. People, please keep your anger in check. Please, no more updates about bludgeoning your adulterous ex-wife, and please, no more updates about how your ex-husband's private parts always looked like he just came out of a cold pool. Your status updates are not your therapy journal.

165 > Don't tell me who I should know, Facebook

Blogger Rex Sorgatz (who, according to Gawker.com is "the media's favorite expert on microcelebrity") hit the nail on the head when he said, "The 'people you should know' list on Facebook is actually a list of people you hate." Take a look and you'll see it's true! It's a collage of all the people in life you couldn't stand.

facebook FACT

Denmark is the world's biggest Facebook fan—34 percent of the population has a Facebook account.

166 > I did know you, until you defriended me

While the "people you should know" list is surely a list of people you don't want to be friends with, the street goes both ways, as you can sometimes find out unexpectedly. Like when you think you had a simple squabble with someone, but you then find out they defriended you because suddenly Facebook thinks you should know them. I do know them! What I *didn't* know is that the jerk defriended me. Now, instead of patching things up in real life, we have this awkward virtual argument that can only be resolved by blocking.

167 > You didn't really like meeting them, but they friended you anyway

Oh, what to do. How I long for the days of the fake smile, followed by a limp handshake and a wan "Nice meeting you." Now those false attempts at appearing enthusiastic don't make you look good because you actually have to deliver. You really need to watch what you say because the next morning could result in an e-mail saying how nice it was to meet you too and a friend request. And then you're stuck with the mayor of Dullsville for life.

168 > Multigenerational "MyFacing"

If you don't know the name of the website you just signed up for, then you shouldn't be allowed to have an account. I knew my world was about to end when my NRA-card-carrying, church-choir-singing, roller-skating-champion aunt joined the site she innocently calls "MyFace." While I do delight in the times she tells the family about how "so and so was on my face," it is a little disconcerting to see her post about how gracious God is while I'm obsessively deleting photos of myself at the annual Drinko De Mayo party. I'm just sayin'.

Daniel is your mom.
47 minutes ago · Comment · Like

---

169 > Pathetic attempts at appearing popular

Here's a tip. When every time you come home from a party you end up with five new "friends" who never end up posting anything to your Wall . . .

ever . . . it just makes you look desperate. It makes you look like you're try-ing to get people to your party. And while they're okay with drinking your booze and eating your food, they don't really remember your name.

170 > Are you really having fun when you're spending the whole night on your phone?

How much fun are you really having if you have the time to constantly post about how much fun you're having? If the party you're at is so damn awe-some, shouldn't you be having an awesome time rather than whipping out your iPhone to update your Facebook status so everyone knows what an awesome time you're having?

Eli It's such a gorgeous day out, I've decided to stay inside, and clean my house

about an hour ago · Comment · Like

---

171 > It sucks when you have more fun than I do

Okay fine, say you *are* having more fun than I am. Do you need to rub it in? And do you ever plan on inviting me to any of those Sunday morning beach bocce parties? Or how about the Drunkpocalypse party of your friends that I kinda sorta know? Or are you sitting at home just like I am trying, pretending you actually have fun on Friday nights? 'Cause if that's the case, I'll share my case of PBR with you.

172 > Happy birthday message BS

As if birthdays needed to be any more stressful. Now you not only have to worry about getting closer to collecting social security, but you need to worry about whether people will post birthday wishes to your Wall . . . which really causes us to take a giant step backward. Remember the stress of your seventh birthday, when your mom planned that big shindig with the special cake and the magician and no one showed because Disney on Ice was in town? It wasn't because they didn't like you. Honest! And if no one posts to your Wall, it must be because there's something big going on over at Twitter. It has nothing to do with you. I swear to God.

173 > No one calls you on your birthday anymore

As though the public scrutiny of your birthday wasn't bad enough, people now think that a posting on your Facebook page is enough of a birthday well-wish that nothing more is required. Now, we're all adults here; we don't need people to fall all over themselves to wish us a happy birthday. But when your voice mail is conspicuously empty on your birthday, it can certainly make you feel like crap.

174 > The paranoia of overposting (am I doing it?)

Oh, God. Am I "one of those people"? Am I? One of those people that all of their friends "hide"? I have so much to say! I love to share and once upon a time I thought Facebook was for sharing, but then I overheard conversations about the annoying people who overpost and now all I can do is worry that I'm one of them.

facebook FACT

Psychologists in the United States have diagnosed a new condition: FAD (Facebook Addiction Disorder).

175 > I hear about Facebook on the street

I finally pull myself away from my computer long enough to take a walk, and what happens? I end up hearing a group of people talking incessantly about Facebook at the ice cream stand. This is ice cream! Pay attention to the delicious sweet creaminess before you. If even an amazing ice cream cone can't get the attention of the human race, then I think we're stepping into seriously dangerous territory.

176 > Deleting old postings to look cool (I've done it)

I'm loath to admit it, but when you post a good status update, it's so validating. It's like a public pat on the back when people tell me I'm funny or witty or pretty or that they want to buy me presents just for being me. It really helps me get over my insecurities. I even sometimes post from my cell phone, but I can't look overeager. So once every few days I go through my Wall and make sure I delete old posts, so as not to look too attention-starved or needy. That way I'm both wildly attractive and hopelessly unavailable.

Tony would lose his mind if it weren't attached.
5 hours ago · Comment · Like

---

177 > 25 Things (the pressure!)

I am so sick of 25 Things. That was soooo January 2009. And yet they are still circulating and, as time goes on, people are getting wittier and wittier. And that makes one of the trendsetters (me) look like an overly earnest ass. And that sucks. I see no other alternative than to update my 25 Things to look as awesome as all the Johnny-come- latelies who had an unfair advantage after reading about a million of these posted over the course of a few months. And do I feel bad about it? No. As a matter of fact, updating my 25 Things is one of my favorite things. So there.

178 > When you post on my Wall and then "Like" what you posted, you look like an idiot

The problem starts with the fact that you've posted so much crap on my Wall that it looks like a bombed-out neighborhood in Tehran circa 1982. You post a million videos, photos, and links that clog up my page, and my computer goes into such a frenzy I can't even delete them. And then . . . you "Like" them. Yeah, no kidding. One might assume that if you search for something and then are moved to share it, you like it.

179 > Who the hell is that guy they keep suggesting as a friend?

Do you see him too? Who the hell is that guy? He's like the peeping Tom of my computer screen. I'm just trying to keep tabs on my friends and show the world how witty I am through bitchin' status updates, but that guy is always looking over my shoulder. Do you see him too? I want to delete him from the "People You May Know" list, but Facebook knows all and Facebook seems to think we're BFFs or something. What if I delete him and find out that this was the friend I'd been looking for all my life? God, I hate that creepy sonofabitch.

180 > When you find out the weird girl from high school is actually crazy but—too late—you already friended her

The advice works for boyfriends and it works for Facebook friends: People do not change. Ever. Don't think that just because ten or twenty years have gone by since high school that that person who was wackadoo then has somehow turned into the coolest person on the planet and your psychic soul sister. Because she hasn't, she is still insane, only now she's pretending to be your insane BFF, manically responding to and "liking" every darn thing you post. Because BFFs are nothing if not supportive—even insane BFFs.

181 > Your reputation is at stake

I really resent the fact that Facebook has destroyed my potential to be a totally awesome role model. I feel I should get to reserve the right to drink my face off, flash my boobs, and flip the bird to a security guard in the privacy of my own drunken stupor. Whatever happened to the halcyon days of keeping your semipublic humiliation between friends and the police notes? Now they're there for all to see and, quite frankly, marvel at. And if you don't log in for twenty-four hours and you miss the postings, it's like a horrible game of telephone gone berserk.

182 > Slicing and dicing the friend pie

Friends, family, coworkers. This is where everything gets a little shady. My plan was just to have an online book of faces—or whatever the heck Facebook hoped for—but now I have this highly uncomfortable meeting ground of worlds that should really remain separate. While my high school friends may think it hilarious to reference the time I fell down the stairs and my skirt flipped over my head in front of most of the basketball team, I'm thinking that's not the best way for my boss to view me. Just sayin'.

183 > The random girl you met at a party

Come on! I just met you. You seemed so nice and I'm sure we would have been friends in due time, but now you go and friend me and I feel like I can't say no. Okay, nice girl I met at the party who could potentially be a really good friend, now that you've friended me, where does that leave us? I get to see in my friend feed all of the fun stuff you're doing but since we don't even know each other beyond a twenty-minute chat, I can't rightly say, "Hey, that party you're going to next week looks fun. If you need a cohort . . ." No, I can't. You know why? Because that would make me look like a stalker. Great. You started it—*you* friended *me* and now I'm the stalker?

184 > The new media addict

You are such an annoying hipster. Let me be blunt: I cannot stand that you friended me without barely knowing me. And I cannot stand your TinyURL updates that you post every forty-five minutes. Look, I get it. I get that you love new media and you think Facebook is a "powerful networking tool." We all get it. But just how effective is Facebook for your evangelism if I hide you? That's right, you're at code orange and . . . oh, wait. Too late. Hide.

Ryan is out of this wet coat and into a dry martini!
5 minutes ago · Comment · Like

(Author's note: Ryan is gay, in case you didn't know.)

185 > But I wanted to defriend you first!

Wait a minute. WTF? I had 319 friends yesterday. Why am I at 318 today? Who the hell defriended me? And why? I'm diligent about making sure my postings are both witty and socially pertinent (that *Flight of the Concords* video totally ruled), and IMHO, my status updates are hilarious. Why would someone defriend *me*? Maybe it was a former boss . . . no . . . maybe . . . WAIT A MINUTE! Not my "mercy make-out" from college. You do *not* get to defriend me. That is NOT fair! I wanted to defriend you first. Where do you get off? Oh, well two can play at that game. Block. Yeah, you heard me. You're blocked! How d'you like me now?

Angelina Oi.... Epic taco hangover... pics tomorrow.
36 minutes ago · Comment · Like

---

186 > Silent but deadly

Sly defriending requires all of the stealth of MacGyver, combined with all of the feigned self-righteous kindness of a fallen televangelist getting ready to go to court. You need to be able to sneak out of the room as softly as a mime, but you can't totally be a mime, because then you'll get your ass kicked. The silent defriending is to be handled delicately. First, you "hide" the person so as to emotionally detach from them. You can't second-guess yourself; the slaying must be swift. Then you stop commenting on their page and stop responding to any Facebook communication they send your way. Make them think you died or something; that's a process I find to be most effective. The last step is where you really need to look deep within yourself to figure out what you want to achieve with the defriending. Do you want to inflict mortal pain? Then a simple defriending will do. But if you truly want to cut off all ties, a block is the better choice. The block is the Facebook equivalent of falling off the face of the earth.

187 > How do you have time to skulk around, waiting for me to say something stupid?

Honestly. Do you *ever* log out of Facebook? Ever? And while you're on Facebook, do you just sit there waiting for me to say something stupid? I mean, I know you are highly educated, you read three newspapers a day, follow all the political wonks and can talk endlessly about public policy. You know what, though? Every now and then a girl is entitled to make a joke. Cut me some slack. Rule of thumb, if every post you make starts with "actually," it means you're pompous jerk. Plain and simple.

Chapter 11

It's High School, All Over Again

188 > There's a *reason* I never kept in touch with her

When she beat me up in the fourth grade, I figured we had some stuff to work through if we were ever going to be BFFs. When she threw me into the locker in the tenth grade, I could tell we weren't going to be friends. When she outed my bra size at the top of her lungs for the whole high school to hear—that was when I decided I hated her. I've spent my whole life trying to avoid her, so WHY is she friending me on Facebook? What if I ignore her friend request and she gets angry and starts posting my bra size in her status updates and I never know? But then what if I do friend her and then she convinces SuperPoke to create a "throw into a locker" option.

189 > The high school friending flurry

Wow, it's like a tsunami from everyone who ever destroyed your self-esteem or humiliated you publicly. It's like a friending flurry of people you're pretty sure always hated you and who definitely want to see you fail. You go away for a weekend and suddenly your whole high school class is on Facebook. And they've all found you. And they all want to know if you finally got your braces off. You like some, you don't like others, and you can't even remember who the rest of them are. But you have no choice. If you friend one, you need to friend them all. So get ready to look like a total needy a-hole with a 20 percent surge in friends. Apparently, peer pressure never gets old.

Sondra blueberry milkshake!!!
3 hours ago · Comment · Like

---

190 > There's only so much rah-rah hometown horseshit one person can take in a lifetime

How many Facebook groups can be devoted to one town of less than 30,000? We have a group for if you were born in Gloucester, Massachusetts, a group for Gloucester Potholes, a group for if you were a student at Gloucester High School but didn't sign a pregnancy pact, and on and on. I love my hometown, but am I really supposed to join all of these? I didn't make the cheerleading squad for a reason. It's because I'm genetically predisposed to not give a rat's ass. Just because a few years went by doesn't mean that's gonna change.

191 > When the prom queen points out that you still "look single"

Let it be known that when the prom queen, who has 2.5 kids, a station wagon, and a chocolate lab, just as she always planned, says, "You look like you're having so much fun. I'm living vicariously through you," she isn't being any more gracious now than she was in high school. She is judging you. She is looking to see your relationships status and she is gossiping with the whole damn prom court about how she always knew you'd never get married. It's okay though. The reason she only posts photos of her kids is because she got fat. Just write her back and say, "Damn, you look *healthy*." Works every time.

192 > Why you'll regret being friends with the editor of your high school yearbook

The worst thing you can ever do is be friends with the editor of your high school yearbook. Why? Because, mark my word, she not only stole a handful of photos too humiliating to actually run in the yearbook right before graduation, she still has them. And she knows exactly where they are. And if she hasn't already scanned them in, she's doing so right now. And she is a terrible awful person for it. No one needed to see the photo of you wearing headgear freshman year then, and they sure as hell don't need to see it now.

193 > My pathetic high school yearbook gone public

And on the subject of yearbooks. There's a reason why my yearbook has sat in a closet for more than a decade; it's because it was pathetic. Facebook sucks because it resurrects the same, precise feeling of not getting your high school yearbook signed by anybody while watching everyone else proclaim their love for each other. You get to have that good old outcast feeling right at the tip of your fingertips now, twenty-four hours a day, seven days a week. Isn't the Internet efficient?

194 > Cliques, hazing, and social hierarchies

Social networking my ass. This is more like Outsider 2.0. How is it possible that long after high school has ended you can still find yourself excluded from the popular clique? People still top friend and people still start groups where they talk about things you have no idea about because you weren't invited to the party. I'm beginning to wonder if Facebook is actually about bringing people together or simply alerting them to the fact that they never fit in and they never will. So basically, if you were a mean girl in high school and you've since mellowed out, Facebook will remind you how to passive-aggressively catapult yourself back into the alpha role. When you want to make others feel like shit, creating a top friending is always a popular choice. Let your friends know who your BFFs are—and who sits on the second tier.

Dissed from the prom court, baby? Don't worry, you get to relive that night all day every day on the Interwebs.

195 > Girls' room gossip and juicy breakups

Ooooooh, this is better than meeting in the girls' room for a smoke. Beth and Dave totally broke up at 7:00 last night and within an hour he was listed as "In a Relationship" with Sarah. This is just like passing notes in class, only way better because it's totally "verified." The only downside is that it's hard to be the Alpha Gossip when everyone gets the same info at the same time. That's why I totally need an iPhone. There must be an app for this?

Karin can't. stop. eating.
29 minutes ago • Comment • Like

---

196 > When couples fight via status updates

Talk about awkward. When someone posts that her husband is "a selfish prick" on her page and then her husband posts "Jim is sleeping on the couch," we're getting a little glimpse of reality that we just don't want to see. A good rule of thumb is, if something is awkward when you say it in public at lunch, then it's probably going to be awkward when you post it in your status update. And when people "Like" it, that's just their way of trying to change the subject. They don't want to hear more. They want you to see a marriage counselor.

197 > Couples who share Facebook accounts

Nothing says you're in a needy, co-dependent, and symbiotic relationship like a joint Facebook account. The only time such things should be allowed is if the two people sharing an account are eligible for AARP benefits and if one of them is a total Luddite. If you are a couple in your twenties, thirties, or forties, this is completely unacceptable and essentially the Web 2.0 equivalent of one control-freak spouse talking for the other.

Chapter 12

Why Picking the Perfect Profile Pic Is like Picking a Prom Dress

198 > Less than 2 percent of all pics posted were taken in this decade—what the hell do these people really look like?

Well, this is kind of odd. You're posting photos from when we took algebra together? Considering you have since graduated from college and went on to get your PhD, I'm assuming you've had a few more experiences since then notable enough to have your picture taken. I'm not calling you old or anything, but a lot of time has passed since the ninth grade. And I think I heard you're married, so I'm guessing you've got a more recent photo or two kicking around. Or is this one of those things like you'd rather we "remember you as you were"?

facebook FACT

There are more than 500 million private photos on Facebook . . . and counting!

199 > Tag, you're it!

Photo tagging totally sucks. Actually, being the recipient of a photo tag might be the single greatest reason not to join Facebook. Your friend who makes you take a dozen "candid" shots together at a party to make sure her double chin doesn't show up is the same friend who will post a photo of you beaming with spinach between your teeth. They shouldn't even call it tagging; they should call it tasing, because almost every time I see a new photo tagged of myself I am temporarily stunned and incapacitated. Right up until I untag that thing and vow to dig up and tag an unflattering pic of the poster.

200 > You think your profile pic makes you look ironic and hip, but it really just makes you look like an idiot with too much time on your hands

Wow. That's quite an angle on that photo. And you've done some mad photo editing. How long did it take you to do that? A simple snapshot wouldn't have done, eh? Why is that? Is it because you couldn't convey your supreme artsiness with your point-and-shoot? I'm glad we can see how Studio 54 you are deep inside now that you've run your photo through the Warhol-O-Matic feature. Because, you know, none of us have ever seen that before.

201 > Your boyfriend's ex loads a new profile pic every seven days

This would be a clear sign she's trying to get him back—a sign you would have been much happier never seeing. But thanks to the wonderful world of Facebook, you can not only see that your boyfriend's ex comments on every single post he makes, she also changes her profile photo like Lindsay Lohan changes sexual preferences. And, much like Lohan's lesbianism, the constant comments and the continually rotating profile photos are all for show. Thank you, Facebook, 'cause everyone needs constant reassurance that the ex who broke your boyfriend's heart is a way better cyberflirt than you are.

202 > There should be crack code to view the profile of your significant other's ex

It's like waving catnip in front of a kitten's nose. You can see her photo, her friends, and that she Likes certain things, but you can't see the good stuff. If you are listed as being in a relationship with someone, there should be a Facebook rule that you get to see his ex's profile if she posts more than twice on his page after the breakup. Let's face it; Facebook is nothing more than a glorified stalking mechanism anyway. Let's use it for what it was meant for: Getting the dirt on those who make you seethe with jealousy.

203 > People who don't show their faces

Hell-o. This is FACEbook, folks. Face. Book. As in, you need to show us your face. Maybe this is some attempt at self-expression I do not fully understand. Or maybe there is some underlying message you're trying to get across. But when you only have one profile shot and it's of a storm trooper, it makes me wonder if you're either (a) a vampire and you can't have your photo taken or (b) one of those weird voodoo people who believe that having their photo taken steals their soul.

Ashley apparently, the microwave was not meant to replace a clothes dryer... whoops.

47 minutes ago · Comment · Like

204 > Why must you timestamp my photo, Facebook?

We've already established that way too many people friend after the first date, so it pays to be proactive. Like making sure the hottest photos of you are already posted before you even go out. But every now and then life gets ahead of us, and we forget to be manipulative game-players. During those embarrassing times when we inadvertently go with the flow, the darn Facebook timestamp totally outs us. Yes, I loaded a new profile photo the minute I got home from my date—but does Facebook have to announce it to the whole world?

205 > Crappy upload? You're stuck with it

No! I uploaded the wrong version of my photo. I was supposed to upload the one where Brigid looked haggard and tired and I looked positively radiant—not the other way around. This is total crap. Only, in the time it took me to figure out my error four people have already commented on the photo—and some comments were quite amusing. What to do? Lose all of the witty comments my friends made and leave the photo as is, or improve my image on Facebook by starting from scratch? If Facebook had even a little bit of a clue they'd allow us to replace photos when such tragedies occur. Looks like I'll have to delete that one and upload a new one. Sorry, Brigid.

206 > Why isn't there just one version of a photo?

Okay, so Vivien uploads a super-fantastic photo of us at costume party and people love it. Everyone is falling all over themselves saying how great we look. But, since Viv keeps all of her photos private, I want to have that photo in my stream as well. So I "share" the photo by posting it to my profile and saving it to my Wall Photos. All should be awesome. Only, then it gets such a great response I decide it'd be a great choice for a profile photo, so I save it as a profile pic. All seems grand in photo land, until you think about the fact that there are now three different versions of the photo with three different sets of comments made to it. Totally confusing. Not to mention annoying.

207 > And on the subject of photos . . .

Why is it the first photos that come up when someone clicks on your profile are unattractive tagged photos? A little respect would be nice, Facebook. You know, we create photo albums filled with our approved photos. Why aren't those the first photos you see when you click on Janelle's Photos? Why is it the first photos all my friends see are grossly unattractive accounts of me acting like an idiot with my friends? Or are you trying to teach me a lesson about acting like an idiot?

208 > The announcement that you've been tagged but you can't see the photo!

This is like being told you have some terminal disease but they're not going to tell you what one. Really, really bad. You get an announcement in your e-mail inbox, which then gets sent to your phone—but you can't click on the photo! You can't see what kind of colossal damage is being done to the way you are viewed by the outside world. You're totally screwed, unless you can get your friend to leave the bar early so you can get to the nearest computer to see the photo. It's the only way.

Lucy My mouth is on fire....and I like it! :-)
2 hours ago · Comment · Like

209 > When people overcomment on your photos

It's really nice when people comment on your photos, but when the comment string goes on and on, it begins to get a little uncomfortable. What am I supposed to do? Are you supposed to sit there and let them talk as though you haven't seen the comments, or should you trim down the comments so as not to appear narcissistic? It's all so complicated. Especially when you post a photo where you think you look nice and then all those weird people who you aren't really friends with and you forgot were even on Facebook start posting four or five uncomfortable observations. That's just awkward.

210 > Skanky photos of girls you used to babysit

What a shame to find some lovely child whose ass I wiped as a penniless teenager has turned into a total ho. Suddenly, that butt that I only remember as being under a pair of pampers and then Carters' is now out there for all to see under that belt she's trying to pass off as a miniskirt. It truly breaks my heart to see you've come to this. But what breaks my heart even more is when my boyfriend walks by the monitor and says, "Whoa, hey! What's her name?"

211 > Those stretched-out webcam photos

Agh! I do not want to see up your nose or see thirty years into the future after your face has been stretched beyond recognition from too much plastic surgery. Those webcam photos need to go away, but people just keep taking them and loading them. At first I figured everyone who did it was high, but then I realized that people who could not possibly be high, like my parents, were doing it. It became a full-fledged fright phenomenon. It's horrifying. It's nasty. It makes you look like you have fetal alcohol syndrome.

Jen ssssshhh! it's a surprise party :)
about an hour ago · Comment · Like

---

212 > Friends who use pictures of their pets as their profile shot

It's a ridiculous trend anyway to post a photo of your pet instead of yourself. Your pet licks its butt; don't let a photo of a face that's spent hours between its own legs be the first thing people think of when they think of you. But if you must post a photo of your dog, cat, bird, ferret, or lemur, please make it a good one. Don't make it one of those gawdawful photos taken with your cheap phone cam, which looks like it's been pre-smeared with your pet's drool.

213 > Friends who use pictures of their food-stained kids as their profile shot

Don't get me wrong, kids are cute. I love kids. I even love your kid when he has strained peas all over his face and when he dumps his diaper out on the couch. A lovable cute and dirty mess and I wouldn't have it any other way, but cut the kid some slack! One error in judgment, like giving himself a pureed sweet potato and corn facial, and suddenly whenever someone thinks of you that's what they see. Which begs the question: What are you trying to hide? Let's see your mug, instead of your kid's.

Chapter 13

Office Facebooking

214 > When your boss friends you

Bosses and employees should never be friends on Facebook. Ever. It can only end badly. Option A is your boss finally figures out you're pretty much a slacker and likely deserve to be fired when she sees you were actually late for a meeting because you needed to finish posting your photos from your trip to London. Option B is you don't end up making yourself look bad, but your friends do when they post lewd responses to your status updates. And Option C is you just never go on Facebook when you're at work, which is totally insane since the whole darn point of Facebook is to have something else to look at besides gray cubicle architorture.

215 > When your assistant friends you

What did I just tell you?! Bosses and employees should NEVER be friends on Facebook. That goes both ways. Don't try to be hip by accepting your assistant's friend request because once he sees your "other side" he'll use it to turn on you. You think it's bad to have your boss see what you're doing? Mark my word, having your assistant as a friend on Facebook is far worse. Because someday that assistant isn't going to like a task you give him, or he's going to want a raise or time off or something where having the ability to unfairly hate on you about personal stuff will be the only thing that makes him feel better when you say no. Consider yourself warned.

216 > Coworkers on Facebook

This *seems* like an innocent and fun way to keep things light between coworkers. But do you really want your coworkers to see photos from the beach getaway you took last weekend? And do you really want that creep in the next cubicle to monitor your relationship status? Coworkers as friends on Facebook add a whole new meaning to "socially awkward."

217 > The company network

Now this is where you're trapped. The company network. This is where you're invited to join a network of all your peers with the profile you've been using to keep up with your high school and college friends. Worlds collide, and they do so like a deck of cards falling down. And here we've got the ultimate case of damned if you do and damned if you don't. Don't join the network and everyone will wonder why. But once you join that network you make yourself instantly vulnerable, so think before you click. You know how embarrassed you are that your friends are seeing tagged photos of you dancing toward the championship in the Macarena dance competition. Think of how much more awesome things will be when your CEO sees those photos too.

Andy Friend me on Skype and we can video chat for no reason. It'll be awesome.

32 minutes ago · Comment · Like

---

218 > HR stalkers (they *do* check your profiles)

You need to be smart about this because, really, there's only so much I can do to save you. You know when the village wench starts posting on your boyfriend's page you go into mad stalker mode and page through all of her photos and then click down her Wall until the beginning of time to see if he's posting back? Anyway, you do that because you're temporarily insane, but HR people are actually PAID to get the dirt on you. You follow me? They are absolutely going to look for your Facebook account. And when they see the ill-selected profile shot of you doing body shots off your neighbor they might not consider you quality employee material. Just sayin'.

219 > It's hard to ignore a company party invite when your boss sees you've updated your status

Oh no. See, I TOLD you not to friend your boss and now you have screwed yourself. I have no sympathy for you. You were so good about not posting status updates ever since last Wednesday, when she sent out the invite to the team-building spinach-eating party at the local Elks Club. But then, with only two days to the event, you spaced and did another freaking 5 Things list and totally blew your cover. Looks like we know how you're spending your Friday night, Popeye. Mind if I call you Popeye?

220 > When your company makes you start a Facebook group

That's right. Let's get right on this bandwagon. Just like with the blogs. It's not like having a Facebook group is a bad idea, but there is such thing as oversaturation. When you have a website, a blog, a listserve, a message board, and a Facebook page (not to mention a latent MySpace page), all you're doing is confusing people. People aren't feeling more connected; they are feeling overwhelmed and unsure of where to best get the information they need. But what do I know? I'll just go back to my cubicle and shut up.

221 > Fired for Facebooking

Did you read about the Swiss woman whose company created a fake account to spy on her Facebook activity? Your boss is going to do the same thing. Well, maybe not exactly the same thing, but your boss is going to find out that you spend four hours a day on Facebook and that's going to get you laid off. Trust me.

222 > But really, I was just listening to iLike

Oh no! I swear this isn't what it looks like. I know your husband told you the same thing when you caught him sleeping with his secretary six months ago, but this *really* isn't what it looks like. I know that every time you walk by my cubicle it looks like I'm surfing Facebook but I swear, all I'm doing is listening to music. Damn Facebook, why can't you get my back for once? Why can't you at least make the iLike pages a different color or something? Now I'm totally going to get laid off and it's all your fault. [Editor's note: Janelle was, in fact, laid off just prior to writing this book.]

223 > Should I status update about how much I hate my job?

In a word? No. Unless you totally want to get fired, keep it to yourself.

Tricia is so excited and she just can't hide it.

3 hours ago · Comment · Like

224 > Status updates about layoffs (also not a good idea)

Want to know how to start a widespread panic? Facebook about your company's layoffs as they happen. Nobody actually works anymore anyway, they're all Facebooking and obsessively refreshing to see if their latest flame has updated their relationship status. Perfect for a captive audience. And a perfect time to freak people like me out. I logged in to Facebook to escape my cubicle, not to be informed that it's possible I'll be thrown out of it. Suddenly the gray cubicle walls seemed so soft and welcoming, just like a mother's arms.

225 > My boss read my timestamp

What did I tell you? Do not friend your boss. Your boss will see everything you do and know exactly when you do it. Don't think he's not paying attention. He hates his job just as much as you hate yours and he's on Facebook just as much as you are. Only thing is, when productivity is down and heads need to roll, it'll be your head on the chopping block. Don't think a simple post saying "Eating a clementine" at 3:15 P.M. is innocuous. You should have been taking that time to file your TPS report!

226 > When friends obsessively update about their awesome vacation and you're in your cubicle

I never thought I'd say I miss the days of old-school slide shows, but I do. I miss sitting around with a group of people looking at vacation photos on a Sunday night. While it seemed like the utmost torture to have to give up time I could have spent watching *The Simpsons,* it pales in comparison to the real-time torture I feel now. I can almost taste your piña colada as I sip my company's free instant coffee. I can almost feel the sun on my face, as I twitch under my office's florescent lights. It's no wonder this virtual vacation leaves me with the feeling of sand in my crotch.

Chapter 14

The Facebook Follies: Dating in a Fishbowl

227 > The dreaded relationship status

I think I need professional help. It's gotten to the point where the Facebook relationship status holds more weight for me than any verbal agreement. Is someone really committed to you if they won't say it on Facebook? Should that be a litmus test for a person's loyalty to you? Or is Facebook just becoming the adult's Trapper Keeper and is your relationship status field just the equivalent to my writing, "Janelle hearts So-and-So"? Sometimes I swear that's what it feels like.

228 > When Facebook announces your breakup

Seems innocent enough. When I update my favorite movies and music, it goes off without any fanfare, but when I decide to hide my relationship status all 300 of my friends and acquaintances see this pathetic broken heart next to my name. Dude, I dumped HIM. It'd be decent if I could tell my close friends before Facebook announces it to the whole world. But if Facebook must be the town crier, couldn't it at least give me a choice of icons? Like, instead of a pathetic broken heart, how about an icon of Oprah giving me the thumbs-up?

229 > When your mom sees your new SO is a fan of Latex and Suicide Girls

Yeah, that one took a lot of explaining. Actually, it took a lot of lying, and my mother still hasn't recovered.

Jon is Wednesdaying.
5 seconds ago · Comment · Like

---

230 > Now when I try to Google-stalk people I get a bazillion returns and about half of them are links to Facebook profile pages

While Facebook has done a great thing in advancing the fine art of cyber-stalking, if a person's account is private, it really creates a conundrum. It makes things much more labor intensive—and, quite frankly, daunting—when you Google someone's name and it comes back with a hundred returns, thirty of which are links to their friends' Facebook pages. That you can't see . . .

231 > When they friend you BEFORE the first date

The only thing worse than someone friending you after the first date is someone who friends you before the first date. Listen, you're not my friend; at this point you're just some person I may or may not be attracted to and who could either be unassailably awesome or unequivocally annoying. If you stood a chance of being the former, you totally blew it by friending me before we even got a chance to show off our plumage on the first date. If you friend me, don't pretend you're not looking at my profile, 'cause I know you are. How on earth am I supposed to make this big white box my plumage?

232 > Unwanted Wall flirtations

Well, here is an interesting dilemma. When someone you know is totally gross starts leaving flirtatious messages on your Wall, do you delete them, or do you use them as bait to appear more attractive to the possible premature frienders. A premature friender can strike at any point, so it's always good to be prepared. Of course, you will need to buy an extra bottle of Tums to get past the stomach-lurching flirtations of said gross guy.

233 > Guys who mean it when they use LOL or TTYL

There should be a support group for people who thought they were dating someone completely normal, only to find out they've gotten involved with an avid LOLer. An occasional OMG can be interpreted as sarcasm and the random BTW can be brushed off as someone in a hurry, but when someone uses LOL or TTYL without a shred of irony you know you've got a dork in your midst. Don't be surprised to see their relationship status gets updated to "I can haz grlfrenz."

234 > When they post photos of themselves lifting their shirt or flashing the peace sign

Admit it. You knew they weren't your type anyway. You passed off their Phish obsession by saying to yourself and your friends that the Phish guys are really good musicians. But it never works to lie to yourself because the truth always rears its ugly head. Like when you see your latest flame frolicking in a muddy field with other "Phans" half his age, flashing a peace sign at the camera.

235 > The Facebook "web of heartache"

What's worse than seeing your ex on Facebook regularly? Seeing your ex friending your other exes, or finding out that your most recent ex is best friends with your previous ex's sister. It's a small world after all, and whether we like it or not we're a species prone to get caught up in six degrees of separation. Once you figure out you have a "type," you're going to find yourself dating that type again and again. And unless you stop playing the field—or begin blocking your exes—you're going to see just how small this world is when you discover that your former beau has moved in with your high school sweetheart's bro. Or worse, when your ex becomes roommates with your most recent one-night stand.

236 > Facebook breeds stalkers

You know it can only end badly and still you stalk. It gets to the point where logging in is enough to torture you. You see their profile photo, floating in your Friends of Friends list—and you know they allow people in their network to see their profiles. So you click. What's a little click? You'll only do it once, you tell yourself. Just a taste. Then you find yourself clicking in every time you log in to Facebook. You find yourself logging in just to see what they're up to. This thing is like an illicit drug! Betty Ford might consider opening her doors for the likes of us.

Morten wondering for how long I would have to train to go to the olympics!?!?

5 seconds ago · Comment · Like

---

237 > Finding out your ex's ex has been Facebook-stalking you

Honey, you better get that profile in lockdown mode because if you think you're the only stalker on this planet, you are sorely mistaken. Like it or not, we're all nut jobs and if you've been stalking someone because you know his name, his network, and what he looks like, you can bet your sweet ass the same is being done to you. Your choice is to take the sane route, making your profile supremely private; or you can take the fun route, posting a million photos in which you are SO having the time of your life, particularly ones that are überflattering in a bathing suit. I'm a big fan of the fun route.

facebook FACT Facebook was launched in February 2004 by Harvard dropout Mark Zuckerberg (who was nineteen years old). By the end of the month, more than half of the undergraduate population at Harvard was registered on the service.

238 > Those who obsessively friend members of the opposite sex

This is so transparent. He goes to a party on Saturday and by Wednesday he has ten new friends, all of the female persuasion. This screams a few things: low self-esteem and douchebaggery. Yeah, pal, thanks for friending me and saying how great it was to meet me. But there were only fifteen people at this soiree, so I know how little time you spent talking to each of us. In fact, it seems as if you exerted more effort to find my name on Facebook than you did trying to make any meaningful connection with me, or the other nine girls you just added to your Friend List. So what's really going on? Is your ex watching?

239 > The crazy new flame who starts friending your parents

Premature friending be damned! This is the be-all end-all of WTF on the Facebook dating front. Nothing says insanity like a new flame friending your parents. There needs to be a definitive time frame in the Facebook rule book for such things. Like, you do not friend my parents until you have had dinner with them at least 2 million times.

240 > Finding out your ex is a total a-hole

We so want to be happy for our exes. I think we all really do. But when his fiancée posts a dozen photos of her engagement ring and the cheapskate never so much as bought you flowers, it's a little too much to bear. Where the hell is the "kick him in the nuts" SuperPoke option?

241 > But I like surprises

Whatever happened to conversation? Now you go on a date with a guy and he already knows everything about you. It's sweet that they take interest in your activities, interests, and 25 Things, but dang if it doesn't get frustrating that, thanks to Facebook, there's no more element of surprise in the realm of dating. And then there comes the awkward moment when he's able to quote back all 25 Things and you have to admit you didn't even know he had a 25 Things list. Hope you brought some extra cash, babe, 'cause you've failed. Looks like you'll be hailing a cab to get home.

242 > Crushes who read too little

Mmmrrppphhhfff. You don't need to memorize my list of favorite movies, but it would be somewhat flattering if you noticed the birthday wishes on my Wall and added one yourself. And, honestly, when I post a really groovy note or link, it'd be nice if you acted a little bit interested. Maybe this should be in that list of thingies that let you know when "he's not that into you." For example, if he's too busy friending a dozen new women a week to read your Facebook page, he's not that into you.

243 > Allows you to keep tabs on your ex

Because of Facebook, you can't really have amicable breakups anymore. Well, you can, but it's not advisable. You need a blowup that will register a 10 on the Richter scale so it's acceptable to defriend. Instead, you're forced into a daily torture chamber the likes of which the Chinese are kicking themselves for not inventing. Now you get to see your ex post 2,000 photos where he's having an awesome weekend with the guys. Without you. And all you want to do is click Remove From Friends, but for some reason that's considered "bad form." Emily Post needs to get 'er done and write up an etiquette book for this.

244 > OMG, the a-hole defriended me!

And speaking of Emily Post, how the hell do you handle it when the aforementioned ex defriends you first—and does it without warning. Don't you agree there should be some sort of polite farewell e-mail or something? Shouldn't that be a requirement for any person you let touch your boobs? Especially when you planned on defriending him first and the only reason you didn't is because you couldn't find him in your Friend List to do the same. How rude!

245 > Blocking: It can feel so good— as long as you do it first!

But, if he does defriend you first, there are measures you can take to feel vindicated. My favorite is the block. Remember the first time you hit a home run in softball? The crack of the bat against the ball, then it just went sailing and you never felt so free. A good block feels just like that, only better. Remember, Facebook isn't just about connecting with people, it's about sharing. Like sharing with some people that, really, you just don't want to be their friend—virtual or otherwise.

Julie is running out of witty things to say.

11 minutes ago · Comment · Like

---

246 > When your friends won't unfriend him

Don't tell me he's a nice guy. Because he's not! He's actually a total scumbag and I want all of my friends to agree with me on this. In the past your friends could sit silently, nod, and enable you to drown your sorrows in a pint of Chubby Hubby. You thought you were supported. Now, however, you can call them on it when they refuse to defriend him. Attila the Hun used to behead those who were neutral. Now you have the tools to help you do the same. (In case you're wondering, it's called the Block function!)

247 > Being friends with all your exes

This should be filed under "seemed like a good idea at the time." Being friends with your exes seems smart when you're doing it. And in the age before Facebook, it was. You had an anonymous group of guys you ran around with in a previous life but it was a more nebulous group. They were never really defined, they just sort of floated out there. Facebook, on the other hand, gathers them all together neatly. And, what's worse, they let people search through your friends based on their relationship to you. So now there's this awesome way to flaunt to the world that you did, indeed, date a man who now dresses as a wiener for money.

248 > Nobody writes love letters anymore

I really miss the days when you'd get a sweet little letter or postcard in the mail with little romantic doodles in the margins. Nobody doodles anymore! And that's a darn shame. You're missing a whole part of communication when you never see someone's penmanship and absent-minded drawings. Gad! It kinda makes me feel like I don't even know these people.

249 > Facebook infidelities

Facebook has put you back in touch with people who were supposed to be in your past forever. Like Francesco, the hot Florentine sculptor who used to throw you on the back of his Vespa and bring you to his family's olive grove. That was supposed to be a summer fling, in all its perfection. But suddenly you get an unexpected friend request with a message saying, "You look exactly the same," even though you don't. And without warning you've fallen down the rabbit hole, spending every waking moment on Facebook, jumping every time your significant other rounds the corner. Not that I'm speaking from experience, of course.

facebook FACT

As of mid-2009, Facebook reported having more than 250 million active users (active at least once a month) and more than 900 employees.

250 > When your significant other logs in to your account and changes your status update

That was pretty funny honey when you logged in to my account and updated my status to "Janelle is enthusiastically looking forward to motherhood." Loved that. So did my mom and dad. Now tell me again what am I supposed to do with this stroller?

251 > When friends divorce and Facebook about it

Do you really think it's appropriate to use as a status update "Meeting with the lawyers today. He can have the kids but I'll be damned if he gets the house"? I'm just saying, you might want to hold back a bit because, if this were real life instead of the Internet, you would absolutely be hearing an incredibly awkward silence after you said that.

252 > When your SO's mom uses Facebook to publicly give relationship advice

It's great that your mom is so involved and that she really cares about your personal life. Truly, I think that's a great thing. I just don't think it's cool for a mom to post on her kid's Wall, "I can't help but notice your relationship status hasn't been updated. Don't you think it says something about a person if they won't change their status?" It also sucks when she says, on my Wall,

"I didn't realize you are Italian! You know what happens when Italians and Irish marry! LOL :) :) :)." LOL, indeed.

253 > What happens when his friends are hotter

What a crappy predicament to find oneself in. In the past, you only met a guy's friends when you knew your relationship was solid enough to do so. Now, however, you get a peek at his friends before you're even sure you're interested in the guy. The worst part is being lukewarm about a guy and then finding out that all of his friends are hotter—and wittier—than he is way too early on in the relationship . . . and knowing you most likely can't ask for an intro.

Chapter 15

Power Apps Are for Pussies

254 > I'm going to hide you
if you post one more 5 Things list

The dreaded 5 Things list are the weeds of Facebook. You hide one and ten more pop up in its place. Really, no one cares about the five things you see while seated at your desk. And when you list the five celebrities you've been told you look like, we all know it's just for an ego boost. Especially when, the fact of the matter is, you don't look like David Beckham, you actually kind of look like Chris Farley.

255 > Celebrities I look like

I know it's unfair to pick on just one of LivingSocial's Top 5 lists, but why is it every single woman feels the need to post the Top 5 celebrities she's been told she looks like? And why has everyone, no matter how short, flat-chested, or thin-lipped they are, claim they've been told they look like Scarlett

Johansson? You know what, post it again. Maybe if you just keep saying it your dream will come true. All you gotta do is believe, babe. Just believe.

256 > Putting a gun to the head of Mafia Wars

From Urban Dictionary: "mafia wars: A gay loser game on myspace and facebook it spams your page until your computer crashes it also helps people become internet Gangstas." So, basically, this is spam. Spam asking your friends to follow you on your spamming spree and then follow up by starting a spam family of their own. Don't tell me it's anything different. It's spam, plain and simple. All right, it's tough-guy spam that sprays a fusillade of spam like an AK-47. Is that better?

257 > Okay, fine—I joined the Mafia. But now no one will join MY Mafia!

WTF? I'm sitting here with my Uzi in hand, ready to get on the bandwagon, and now no one will join my Mafia. This game sucks.

258 > I don't even tend my real garden, why would I care about your (Lil) Green Patch?

This is so stupid, I don't even know where to begin. I'm not sure what your li'l green patch is supposed to accomplish, but there's a whole boatload of fresh air outside. Not to mention a ton of grass and green stuff—and if you don't currently have grass or green stuff in your general area, go plant some. Hell, just lay down some dirt and blow a dandelion over it. *Something's* bound to grow.

259 > Wordscraper SO sucks compares to Scrabulous

This is something I, and millions of others, will never get over. The death of Scrabulous. The most perfect, user-friendly, easily loaded, never-ever-crash-your-computer word game that made the workday more tolerable. People joined Facebook just so they could play Scrabulous. It was the perfect online incarnation of the much beloved Scrabble board game, courtesy of developers in India. They mastered a feat that the creators of Scrabble—the board game—somehow couldn't master themselves. So they got all litigious and sued the Indians and made the game go away. Yes, I know it's not fair. Just let it go. We just have to let it go....

260 > You've been invited to play
a word game or chess but you can't spell in real life

This brings up an interesting predicament. To cheat or not to cheat. In real life, cheating take much more finesse than in the cyber world. But in Facebook it's so easy; no one will ever know. And a bazillion cheating websites are immediately at your fingertips. And when the application announces across both your Walls that you won, the stakes are even higher. Just do it. Cheat. Cheating has never felt so sweet.

261 > Do you let them win?

So what if you start dating someone and she asks you to play a game of chess on Facebook and suddenly you find out that she has no strategy for life. A person that dumb won't even be able to navigate her way through the grocer line. What to do? Do you let her win? I'll let you make the call. . . .

262 > You don't really like the person, so should you just let the game die?

This is equivalent to the "slow fade" in a breakup. A person who is interested in you—either as a friend or romantically—challenges you to a game and you are just. Not. Interested. This is where you implement the slow fade. First you take a day or so to even accept their request. Then you pace yourself out, throwing a good week in between turns. This sends a serious message, without actually saying anything. Thank you, Facebook, for helping elevate passive-aggressiveness to a new level.

facebook FACT

120 million users log in to Facebook at least once each day.

263 > But you really just didn't feel like playing!

These stupid apps help breed insecurities, the kind that we never had to deal with in real life. Remember the good old days when someone asked you to play golf but you had other things to attend to? You said something akin to, "Thanks, Bob, but I'm really busy for the next few days. How about we try for another time." You didn't even need to like to play golf. You didn't even need to have any intention of following up for golf, but a friendly smile solved everything. Now, with the assault of application invitations, you have the option of clicking Accept or Reject. No niceties involved. You either go along with it or you flip your friend the bird. Why so black and white, Facebook?

264 > Causes are great, but just because you're a member of ninety causes doesn't mean you're deep

Glad to see you really care. But just so you know, loading the Causes application so you can join a boatload of causes doesn't make you an activist. You see, it's subtle, but the root word in activist is "active." What that means is you will need to take some *action* if you're to prove your commitment to a cause. Oh, look. I see your list already shrinking rapidly. Glad you decided to keep "Equal rights for couch potatoes" on your list. That was an important one.

265 > The hipster challenges

I am not going to out myself as a total music dunce by taking that music challenge. No way am I going to compromise my musical genius status by scoring less than that band geek I friended last week. No way Facebook is outing me. I'll just sit in my cubicle looking cool and aloof and refuse to take the quiz. 'Cause if there's anything less cool than taking a music knowledge quiz, it's flunking it.

266 > When FB tells everyone you're stupid

That's impossible. There is no way in hell I'm only 111 on an IQ test. Jeez, Facebook, if you're going to give me a bogus score the least you can do is hold back a bit until I get a chance to contest it (and totally retake the quiz for a better score). Do you really have to announce it across the newsfeed of every friend and acquaintance I've ever had? Note to self: The intelligent choice is to steer clear of idiotic FB quizzes from now on.

267 > Sorority wars?

I'm kind of tempted by the sorority wars, especially since they told me my seventh-grade boyfriend challenged me. I'm up for the challenge, Caleb. Are you?

268 > IM feature:
You don't know it's there until someone pings you

The first problem with the IM feature is that you always forget that it's there, so you forget to change your status to "offline" (wink, wink). The second problem is that it's nearly impossible to block one person on the list. The third problem is, I'm trying to load up a link to something really important, like Techno Viking, and I get pings from three people asking what I'm up to for the weekend. At least with real IM you had some control. This thing is an introvert's personal hell.

269 > If you want to create a good app,
how about creating something to stream music?!

Ever notice that every Facebook band page seems to link to their MySpace page? True, MySpace is pretty horrible in and of itself, but it has completely trumped Facebook in terms of how to find and stream music and how to tell when a band is coming through your town. When it comes to music, Facebook, I'm cheating on you. And MySpace is sleeping in our bed.

270 > Catbook: Really? A photo isn't enough?

A whole page devoted to your cat? Oh, I get to virtually pet your cat? Okay, I'll bite, but I have to tell you that before I virtually hang with your cat, I need to take some virtual medication for my virtual dander allergies. Gosh, this is such a virtually pleasing relationship. The great thing about virtual pets is their virtual unconditional love. This really makes me so virtually happy. But I have to say that I stop at virtually cleaning the virtual catbox.

Tony is wondering what comes next.

38 minutes ago · Comment · Like

---

271 > WTF? Virtual mini-golf

As though real golf wasn't a sedentary enough sport, Facebook has now made it so you never actually have to get off the golf cart. You can just sit on your rapidly spreading ass and exercise your mouse-clicking fingers all day long.

Chapter 16

The Poke and the *SUPER* Poke: Not as Fun as They Sound

272 > Don't poke me
unless you want to have sex with me

You know. It really annoyed me when my next-door neighbor used to poke me with his finger when we ate lunch. But he grew out of that. I'm hoping that Facebook will someday grow out of this repugnant function. And don't think any of us are missing your witty innuendo, Facebook. We get it.

273 > People poke you to see your profile

Poking should never, never occur between strangers. You need to practice safe Facebooking, and I'm here to tell you how. When a stranger or someone from your past who is not your friend pokes you, they want something more. Poking has become a no-strings-attached way of getting into your profile. You're not some cheap floozy; don't let errant pokers treat you as such.

274 > I tried to be a good sport, but you just poked me again

Poke me once and I'll try to be polite by engaging in a friendly game of "poke the poker." Poke me twice and I swear to God I'm going to lose it. No, I'm not going to block you. I am going to find you in real life and give you a poke in the eye. That's what all this poking has reduced me to.

275 > We're what? Poke buddies? Is this a dating site?

You just listed me as your "poke buddy" in our friendship details. That's not even funny; that's crude. Need I remind you that my NRA-card-carrying, church-choir-singing, roller-skating-champion aunt is on this site? The word "poke" makes her douse herself in holy water. You want that kind of shame on your hands?

276 > Keep that sheep away from me

You just threw a sheep at me? What am I supposed to do with this? Am I supposed to start a knitting circle? Make mutton stew? What am I? Little Bo Peep? Keep your damn sheep to yourself.

277 > If you bitch slap me again, I'll throw my stiletto at you

You know, if you want to get in a Facebook bar fight, I challenge you to bring it on. Go on, bitch slap me. I'll create duplicate accounts and throw a barrage of stilettos at your ass the likes of which you've never seen. It'll be like a freaking grapeshot cannon. Not to mention, I'll friend your mom and bitch slap her. That's right. I'll bitch slap your mom.

278 > How did they not see that the "stabbing" action was taking it too far?

Taking stupidity to the next level: when Facebook allows people to "stab" each other as a SuperPoke option. And they didn't see it coming when a group of angry parents came charging at them. Remember, Facebook was started at Harvard. These guys went to Harvard. That rejection letter doesn't look so sorry now, does it? Eh, you had more fun at state school anyway.

facebook FACT

On this planet more than 5 billion minutes are spent on Facebook every day.

279 > Day-old insults

My FunWall, or SuperWall, or whatever the hell they're calling it these days (because they change the name every third week) came down after my friend Ed wrote "Balls" on it when I was out of town for ten days. And my twenty-year-old cousin saw it. And now I get invited to her college keggers every weekend. I think she wants to get me liquored up so she can take a sharpie to my forehead.

Chapter 17

Life Gone Public: Your Wall, SuperWall, Groups, and Party Invites

280 > Just message me, Okay?

You know, Vivien. When I forgot my thong at your place after my visit, you really could have e-mailed me to ask about it. There was no need to post a photo on my Wall asking, "Is this yours or Kay's?" There just wasn't. Thank you for returning it intact, but a simple e-mail would have done just fine.

281 > Let's keep the inside jokes inside

I'm still not entirely clear on the purpose of the Wall. It seems to have two functions: 1. to make sure everyone knows you got happy birthday wishes and 2. to make sure everyone knows you share inside jokes with the owner of the Wall. But isn't the point of inside jokes that they stay inside? IMHO, there's NO need to post them on my Wall.

282 > What's so *super* about spam?

I'm beginning to think the whole purpose of a SuperWall is so people can send out massive amounts of spam. I give you my e-mail; I give you my Facebook e-mail; I give you my Wall. Now, spam, you need to take over my SuperWall? I feel like I'm drowning under a steaming pile of spam. But I don't want any spam! (Note: That was a Monty Python joke. Get it? No? Google it.)

283 > Why does everyone need to know what party I'm going to?

Once again, Facebook proves itself as both a vehicle for those that feel socially inferior and a superior stalking tool. First of all, I want to politely accept your party invitation, but I also don't need every friendly acquaintance I have to know where I'm going to be on Friday night. Second, did you know that people can search through all the events their friends are attending? For real. Accepting party invites on Facebook is akin to opening up your iCal for the world to see.

Timothy tells of a Sith legend about how Darth Plagueis got killed in his sleep.

about an hour ago · Comment · Like

---

284 > Seeing your ex pop up on party invites as "attending" totally rots

And since I can see what events all of my contacts are attending, I can also see exactly where my ex will be on Saturday. Which means that even though I planned on going to a different party on Saturday, I can't help but plot a pathetic scheme in my head to show up looking way hotter than when we were together. Thankfully, I can also see which ones of my cute friends are free on Saturday night as well, so I can bring some arm candy along as an accessory.

Robb is listening to john tell a story about jaywalking homosexuals.

25 minutes ago · Comment · Like

---

285 > Maybe attending? How about just a yes or no?

Since when did "maybe" qualify as an acceptable response to a party invite? I know this all started with Evite but, Facebook, you're younger and you could have learned from your predecessor's mistakes. A maybe doesn't tell me how much food or drink to buy. You know, we don't all live in California. Some people actually look for a degree of social commitment when planning a party.

286 > People who post excessively about the fun party they went to without inviting you along

Yes, I saw you accepted an invite to that party I, conspicuously, wasn't invited to. I also saw you update from your phone what a great time everyone was having. And thanks for making sure, lest I might have missed all of that, that I saw the copious photos you took of the evening. And thank you, Facebook, for proving to me that I really am a social loser.

287 > Excessive group invites

Groucho Marx said, "I would never join any club that would accept me as a member." I'm sure if he were alive today, he'd say the same thing about Facebook groups. So that means when you invite me to thirty groups in one day, I'm not going to join any of them. I don't care how much fun the Talking Dolphins group is. I'm having a ton of fun alone, drawing on my own SuperWall.

facebook FACT
About 70 percent of Facebook users are outside of the United States.

288 > Why can't I privately join a group?

I really do want to support my breastfeeding friends, but it is kind of embarrassing when your newsfeed broadcasts that you just joined the "Breastfeeding Is Not a Crime" group. I got eleven e-mails after I joined, all asking if I was pregnant.

Chapter 18

Screw Your Virtual Beverages and Hugs, I'd Like to Get Drunk and Laid

289 > How about buying me a drink in real life, you cheapskate

Is this your lame way of flirting with me? You're buying me a "virtual drink." I don't even know how to respond to this. Are you really that much of a cheapskate that you can't buy a girl a drink in real life? Or am I somehow mistaken and we're at a virtual bar and I've been flirting with the virtual bartender all night. Must have been the virtual Tequila; it gets me every time. Do you plan on getting me virtually wasted? I'll give you some advice: Don't waste your time. I don't virtually kiss on the first date.

facebook FACT

In 2008, *Time* magazine named Mark Zuckerberg one of the world's most influential people.

290 > I don't need a virtual hug,
what I need is a goddamn massage

A virtual hug. Now this is rich. Let's try to use Facebook to keep as much emotional and physical distance from each other as possible yet create an application that makes it look like you care. You know what, if you want to hug me, let's make a real-life plan. Dig? If you're too far away to create a feasible plan for said hugging, a phone call where we can hear each other's voices will work wonders. 'Cause you know what I do with virtual hugs? I delete them.

Stacy I got some tartar control toothpaste. I still got tartar but that shit is under control

57 minutes ago · Comment · Like

---

291 > Are you sending me
a cyber cupcake because you think I'm fat?

Are these virtual cupcakes courtesy of Jenny Craig? Snack food is for snacking, not for beholding on my monitor. The first thing that should be done when you get a cupcake is marvel at it from all angles before you lick off a big dollop of frosting, which you then savor before you dive in. While the presentation of these virtual cupcakes is truly divine, licking my monitor sucks. As a matter of fact, my monitor tastes like Windex.

292 > What's up with these New England artifacts? I don't need a piece of the Old Postal Road, thank you.

As you may have gathered thus far, I don't like the whole virtual gift thing. I like real stuff. But if I must get a virtual gift from you I want it to be pretty, sparkly, and frivolous. I don't want a piece of crap historical artifact that I've never heard of. I'm sure the point is to increase solidarity between people from different parts of the country, but getting one just makes me think: Great, another thing to clutter my Wall.

293 > My box

So we all have "boxes" on Facebook. Boys have boxes and girls have boxes. It makes me feel like I'm back in kindergarten with my little shoebox for stuff. Pardon me while I put this nice piece of flair in my "box." Sounds dirty, doesn't it? I guess that's the only thing I like about it. Couldn't they come up with a better name than box?

294 > Jennifer Aniston thought flair was stupid and so do I

Please, just keep your flair to yourself. The whole point of "flair" was that it was stupid. In the cult classic *Office Space*, Jennifer Aniston did not want to wear her flair and she even quit her job, in part, because of the flair. You give me one more piece of flair and I'm going to "express myself" just like she did. That's right. Big fat middle finger. No more flair.

Carolyn Your opinion doesn't matter.
19 minutes ago · Comment · Like

(Author's note: Are you talking to yourself again, Carolyn?)

295 > Virtual pets

This whole virtual pets thing is ridiculous. Do you remember years ago we all used to make fun of the Japanese for those silly little virtual pets they had on keychains? Yeah, they were quite weird and pretty dumb. But this is worse. Facebook has made me pine for the day of the virtual pet on a keychain.

facebook FACT At twenty-four Mark Zuckerberg is the youngest person to appear on the Forbes Top 400 list, with a net worth of $1.5 billion.

296 > Hatching eggs

I got one of those eggs from someone, expecting to have a cute little baby chicken popping around my page, but it hatched into a moose. Since when do eggs hatch moose? And I didn't even get a baby moose. This one is all old and gangly and fully mature. Give me a baby moose or get off my page.

297 > People who friend you and then only use you as someone to dump apps on

The worst thing about apps are the Dump Trucks. The people who you have a vague connection to who, in the end, never respond to your e-mails, never post anything to your Wall (not even a happy birthday), and who never even poke you! All you are is a dumping ground for apps. You join their Mafia War and then you never hear from them again. I'll tell you now, these people will *never* change. Their relationship is a one-way street and they will never treat you as you deserve to be treated. Tell them to find some other schmuck to take advantage of. They're getting defriended.

PART 3

EVERYTHING ELSE: THE ONLINE OUTCASTS

What I don't like online is superficial networking. It doesn't count for anything.

—Seth Godin

Chapter 19

Friendster: Adding "ster" to Anything Means You're Trying Too Hard

298 > Welcome to the Site of the Living Dead

Once upon a time Friendster was the place where web-savvy twenty- and thirty-somethings came together to connect, share photos, share private jokes publicly, and create a public persona for their private lives. Almost ten years later, a click through the pioneering networking site feels like a walk through a post-apocalyptic wasteland, the likes of which would make a pretty creepy Will Smith movie. Seriously, we're talking kinda eerie. Photos that are almost a decade old stare out at you, with relationship statuses and comments frozen in a time before Facebook and Twitter even existed. Friendster has become little more than a time capsule for what was, with pop ads growing over user content like weeds of neglect.

Red Flag for Failure

Force people who are just starting out in a relationship to qualify their relationship as "Complicated."

299 > How to flatten a good idea

Back in 2001, Friendster was *the* place to be when you were supposed to be doing online research for work. You wanted to connect with folks; Friendster was it. But faster than you can say "Betamax" users changed allegiances—and it was pretty much because Friendster got all high and mighty on its users and they turned around and said, "go screw." Friendster was the classy social networking site, while MySpace was the trashy one. Friendsterers would look down their noses at MySpacers, declaring the new kid on the block as "not really my type." But while the clean and austere look of Friendster was something some preferred to identify themselves with, it proved to be its ultimate downfall. Friendster ended up being less about class and more about control—they darn near turned into Nazi Germany, deleting accounts of anyone who crossed the line of self-expression. Well, Friendster, you made your bed; now it's time to lie in it. Look who's saying Achtung now.

300 > Huge in Asia, no kidding

For a few weeks there, I just thought my look was particularly appealing to men in Jakarta. Little did I know that all of those friend requests were a small indicator of bigger things going on in Friendster's online wonderland. Suddenly, Friendster was becoming huge in Asia. Good for Friendster, because lord knows the Americans weren't throwing them a bone.

But while I applaud Friendster for finding their niche, it makes me even less likely to visit my account. Why? Well, I don't know anyone in Asia and—to be perfectly honest—I don't care to know anyone in Asia. See, I have this weird thing about me where I really only feel like we're friends if I've met you in the flesh. And, since I do have a few friends I can meet up with on a semi-regular basis, I'm probably going to use my personal time to hang out with them, rather than trying to muddle through an online conversation in broken English. Call me crazy.

301 > Dating website in disguise?

If Friendster is a "place for friends," then why do I have to give my relationship status? Friendster was a way to connect with people, but damn if it wasn't like a pushy Italian mother—forcing you into dating scenarios, whether you wanted to or not. Personal space be damned, you will use this site as the developers intended or they will close your account.

302 > "How You're Connected"—
the feature *no one* has picked up

One thing I do like about Friendster is the "How You're Connected" feature, which actually did make it a good resource for meeting people. Friendster was the only networking site that actually encouraged you to network. But why is it that no other site has clued into this? With the demise of Friendster, we've watched the baby go the way of the bathwater (and now you'll never be able to find out how you and the baby were connected)!

303 > Whoa! Don't "rate" my photos!

Hey, now! This isn't Hot or Not, this is Friendster. You're not allowed to rate my photos! And who the hell gave my bikini shot only three stars? Totally lame. Friendster forces me to treat this like a dating site, so I throw up a cute photo and then one of my a-hole "friends" gives it a measly three stars. With friends like this, who needs enemies? I'm going to enemy-ster you, you jerk.

304 > They can see I searched for them?!

Friendster is completely ruining my reputation as a stealth cyberstalker. When you see someone's face taunting you to click on his profile, how can you ignore it? You click, with the innocuous intention of learning everything about that person, but then Friendster goes and blabs its mouth off to the whole darn world wide web that you just peeked. I'm *so* not down with this feature. The whole point of stalking is that the person being stalked should never know they're being stalked. Otherwise, you're a peeping Tom—see the difference?

305 > Ancient Friendster e-mail

What Friendster does have is a little notice on everyone's page that says, "Yo! I haven't been here in three months—don't e-mail me." And yet, people still do. Friends still do. People who want to make friends still do. And then, after six months of inactivity, you log in out of morbid curiosity only to find that you have—amidst nine spam e-mails—one lonely e-mail sent from a sweet stranger three months ago saying, "Hey, I'm new in town and don't really know anyone. Seemed like we have some stuff in common so I thought I'd take a leap of faith and get in touch." And then you feel like a total jerk.

Red Flag for Failure

Don't allow for any e-mail notification functions. *(Honestly, I forgot Friendster even existed!)*

306 > Testimonials

The whole testimonial thing was completely humiliating. Thank goodness MySpace and Facebook didn't follow suit. Basically, it asked your friends to tell the world how awesome you are. While some pages had heartwarming statements of how this person touched someone's life, others had unflattering observations such as "Janelle will eat anything I put in front of her. And has been known to consume an entire crown roast in one sitting."

307 > "Full" Friends Lists

Since Friendster was all about being "legit," they had a litany of rules that users tried to get around. One of the most nauseating was the second profile trend. Friendster had its share of needy a-holes whose prime motivation was to accrue as many "friends" as humanly possible. These people tended to have upward of 100 photos on their profile, 90 percent of them scantily clad and having more fun than you would ever care to in your lifetime. But those friends always ended up tapping out the maximum number of friends they could have. So you'd end up getting friend requests from AmandaBliss1, AmandaBliss2, and so on until you basically just deleted your account because Amanda was way too blissful to be your friend.

308 > Friendster caves

After MySpace came around, about the only thing Friendster had going for it was the fact that it had a cleaner, classier format that would download easily. But instead of trying to figure out ways of improving their product, Friendster went the way of the insecure friends and started trying to emulate MySpace in every possible way. Such as allowing distracting homemade background skins—90 percent of which are of the account holder mauling her boyfriend, while Tinkerbell flashes in the corner saying, "Dreams really can come true!"

309 > Friendster allows the "forward" function

While the forward function would be an awesome tool when you're writing to someone you actually know, in the wrong hands it's just a pain in the ass. Like when you get a friend request from someone you don't know from Singapore, so you shoot them a quick Friendster e-mail asking who they are. They end up forwarding it to fifty friends of theirs, saying, "Thank you for add Janelle." And suddenly you're a freaking celebrity. Everyone wants to be your friend and everyone wants to show you the HOTT new video they shot on their webcam. And they all want to see yours too! Because that's what friends do. They share.

310 > I think I'm still on Friendster because I feel bad for it

Bottom line, I'm not on Friendster because I use it—I don't think anyone outside of Asia uses Friendster anymore—I'm on Friendster because I feel bad for it. I don't want to just abandon it. I mean, it seems like a perfectly nice website, it's just pretty useless. When I only had thirty friends on it to begin with (and that's counting Amandabliss1 and Amandabliss2), and seven have dropped off, it makes no sense to log in. But I'll be darned if I leave Friendster out in the cold. Just because the popular girl isn't popular doesn't mean she doesn't have a heart. I mean, she was a total bitch, so I'm not inviting her to my birthday party, but I'll say hi to her in the hallways. You know what I mean?

Chapter 20

MySpace: Rupert Murdoch Must Be Kicking Himself

311 > The school slut of social networking

Poor MySpace. Once everyone had their way with her, they dropped her like an old shoe and went chasing after Facebook, the popular girl in prettier clothes with an Ivy League background. She's a really good kid; she just came from a rough part of town. I just wish she'd have some self-respect. Always dressing in flashy clothes, pulling up her shirt and passing it off as a "pop up," blaring her music every time you visit, and shamelessly copying Facebook at every corner. I know she wants to be friendly, but she's coming off as desperate.

312 > Epilepsy 101: Flash ad overkill

Holy crap, I think I'm going to have a seizure. Flashing lights, blinking ads, and a

Red Flag for Failure

Make a site so busy I can't stand looking at the welcome screen.

million spinny, animated GIFs are causing my brain to short-circuit. After looking at MySpace for more than two minutes I feel like I need to take a nap. This place is a freaking mess. It's like a virtual rave—an optical tornado coming at me, and there is no place to hide.

313 > Elevating profile hacking to an art form

If profile hacking were art, MySpace would be the goddamn Louvre. I have never experienced so much hacking in one place—and so often—in all my life. Whoa, those aren't my tits I just sent you a photo of! I wish they were, but they're not, and I'm really sorry I sent a photo of them and some sixteen-year-old's ass to your account. I'm also sorry that when you clicked on the photo of the ass in question, you were taken to a site that stole all of your personal information and made you look like a slimeball with zero regard for grammar and spelling.

> **Red Flag for Failure**
>
> Make it more hacker-friendly than user-friendly.

314 > Band posting gone bad

While MySpace is still the best social networking site for discovering new music, it's also a place for some bands to act like needy and inconsiderate douchebags. The word "friend" implies a certain level of consideration. Like, you should be polite or at least make a small attempt at social grace. When you use my comments section as a bulletin board for every show you plan to be in, it mucks up my page, makes it hard to load, and makes it so my **real** friends can't even log in to it. That shizzle takes up bandwidth—ain't it ironic that the **bands** of MySpace are stealing all my page's **bandwidth**? Well, pretty boys, if you don't get your act together, yours is going to be one BAND I plan to be WIDTHOUT.

315 > A half-assed attempt to emulate Facebook while still looking as ugly as Joan Rivers between face lifts

MySpace has added "Friend Updates" and the ability to tag people in photos, but it feels slapped together and is still wedged between blinking ads, AdSense, crappy featured profiles, and other nausea-inducing atrocities.

316 > Image-heavy posting

Oooooh my God. Oh my freaking God. Your page is taking so long to load; it's like Eeyore on Quaaludes. I don't know what the deal is with MySpace, but for some reason people feel like they can't have a page without a background, and they refuse to keep their photos where they belong—that would be in their *photo albums*. MySpace lets you create as many as you want. Why do I need to see them all in RAW form, right there as soon as I log in to your page? I'm sure there's some parable of patience in here, but I'm not having it. Slow and steady wins the race, my ass. Slow and steady causes me to shut down your page and go to CNN.com. Okay, PerezHilton.com.

317 > Needing to verify every posting

Red Flag for Failure

Make it more difficult to post a comment to a friend's page than it is to get out of a Colombian prison.

I feel like I need to go through more red tape to post a comment on a friend's MySpace page than I would to fly home from a summer holiday in Saudi Arabia. All I want to do is tell my friend the photo she took is pretty, and now I need to type in a verification code I can't even read and then it's going to take a day for her to decide if she likes my comment or not. I blame this all on the bands. This is all their fault.

318 > Internal errors galore! Seriously, every third click

One. Two. Three. Down. Hang on, this is going to be a bumpy ride. There are few things in life as predictable as MySpace errors, which occur—like clockwork—every third click you make on the site. It'll never let you down; I promise. Heck, it's so dependable you could make a drinking game out of this.

319 > The "last login" update (you can't hide!)

Let me tell you something about MySpace. MySpace is a duplicitous bitch. It will turn on you in a HEARTBEAT. MySpace is not your friend. It does not let you secretly log in to talk to your really cool friends while you totally blow off your lame ones—because

it tells everyone the last time you logged in. It's the freaking town crier, "Yo! Clingy guy she dated in college. Take a look at her last login. Three days ago. She totally got your message and she's ignoring you." Thanks, MySpace, for helping a sister out.

320 > Tells people when you've read their e-mails

And to make matters worse. You can't even say, "Oh sure, I logged in, but I didn't get around to reading your message." Because you absolutely did and MySpace just announced it. Yep, marked as **read**, as in you read his message and you blew him off and you can bet he knows it and you need to come up with something better.

321 > I can't see my friend of friend, but you're recommending pages of perfect strangers

Facebook's recommendations are bad, but MySpace's make no sense at all. Now people on MySpace have started making their pages private, which is their prerogative. No judgment here. But when I can't click on the page of a friendly acquaintance I haven't friended yet, I'd like to know who the heck these people are that you're recommending to me. A sixteen-year-old boy in Alberta? As a thirty-something woman in Boston, I'm not sure what you're implying, MySpace.

322 > You can't get rid of your stupid comment feed

Comments, in my humble opinion, suck. They are just private discussions made public to feed our egos, which social networking sites are secretly aiming to destroy. The fifteen-year-old cousin you probably shouldn't have friended fills comment feeds with bandwidth-draining images, and mind-numbing statements. Yet MySpace holds you to them! It holds you to all of them. And the only way to escape them is to laboriously delete them one by one, which not only offends your cousin, who is totally going through puberty, it makes you kinda look like a dick.

323 > Don't break up with me on my MySpace

Did you know people do this? They do! It's become an acceptable form of relationship-ending behavior. No wonder people have come to obsessively log in to their networking accounts. We can blame it on MySpace! I've actually seen this, and this is what people have to say: "Well, if you didn't end up getting close enough to say it in person and the girl was really disrespectful in a way that his friends should know, then she deserves it." *Thank you*, Dr. Phil.

324 > Birthday bonanza

Past, present, future. Who cares? MySpace certainly doesn't. As long as it's within a one-month radius, it's all good. Today I see notifications for Victor's birthday, which is in three days; Marshall's, which is in two weeks; and Allison's, which was a week and a half ago. I wouldn't be surprised if in a month or two people start seeing notifications for my birthday, which is six months from now. This is when MySpace starts acting like a hippie. Sure, I flaked out on your birthday last month, but I'm saying happy birthday to you now. Don't harsh my mellow, dude.

> **Red Flag for Failure**
>
> Forget that birthdays only take place once a year.

325 > MySpace might be kind of mentally challenged

Sometimes I think MySpace is so caught up in its own ego that it doesn't know its ass from its elbow. How did I get in my own "extended network"? If I look at my profile page, it says "Janelle is in your extended network." That's curious because I know Janelle pretty well. That's because I am Janelle, and that profile you're showing me is actually mine. Poor, simple MySpace. Sometimes you just gotta nod and laugh.

326 > The stupid tagline

"A place for friends." Well, I can tell you I've found a fair number of enemies on MySpace too. How about "A place for friends, enemies, freaks, and pornographers?" That might be more accurate. MySpace's tagline is so feel-good and touchy-feely it makes me want to puke. Everyone is welcome; everyone is good; everyone's a friend. It's so freaking Los Angeles, I kind of can't stand it.

327 > The photo album déjà vu

You could go through this forever. And maybe that's the whole point—but I feel like I need a GPS to navigate my way through photo albums on this site. MySpace's photo albums never give you a heads-up, saying you're on Image 1 of x. Next thing you know, your aimless clicking has you already a quarter through your second go-around before you've realized where you are.

328 > They get the whole house and they give you nothing but a closet

MySpace used to be "a place for friends," but now it's a place for Rupert Murdoch to pimp whatever new TV show, film, or band Fox is trying to promote. They might want to change their name to AdSpace or FoxSpace. Or maybe CrashSpace, since crashing is pretty much all it's good for with all the pop-up ads it features these days. Excuse me, where am I supposed to put my stuff? This is hardly my space, it's Fox's space. Click on my home page and all you see are links to crap I don't give a rat's ass about. It's like moving in with a territorial roommate, you moved in all optimistic, but you're only going to get to use a tiny sliver of the space.

Red Flag for Failure

Call yourself MySpace but provide no space for me!

329 > The good, the bad, the bands

The best part about MySpace is that you get to find a lot of good music you never would have. The worst part is that you find out your friends have really crappy taste in music. The crappier their taste, the more videos and streaming music they post on their pages. Make no mistake, MySpace is on their side—not yours. They let every person, no matter how bad their taste in music, load the little radio thingy that blares out music every time you click on their page. My heart goes out to the person who forgets to turn off their sound when they click to MySpace at the office. What they get is a sonic slap in the face. It's big, it's loud, and more often than not, it's really, really bad.

330 > Thank you for crashing my archaic computer because you had to "express yourself"

I think we can safely blame Los Angeles for this. If MySpace were developed in Boston it would be a staid, cold, emotionally unavailable, and unenthusiastic social networking site that would always load easily and on time and would only be fun to log in to in the summertime. But because it was developed in Los Angeles, it's all about fun, flash, sex, rock-and-roll, and explicit self-expression. Expression that will crash your computer every time you log in to the site. Expression that will give your computer a virus and will give your brain a seizure. It's like a freaking visual STD you can't get rid of.

331 > A place for music

Take a look at any band's Facebook pages and you'll see that nine times out of ten there is a link to the band's MySpace page. While the site may be dying a slow death in other ways, it's still the place where bands get their sounds out to the people. Why does that suck? Because I just want to

Red Flag for Failure

Let teenagers be graphic designers.

delete my damn MySpace account. I just want to be rid of it. I just want to be able to ditch one site, just one. And I can't because once I delete that account I lose the nice little list of bands that I like in my friends list. So my choices are toggle between two sites or try to find every band on Facebook and friend them so I can keep track of touring, announcements, and other goodies. MySpace, it's like you were expressly created to be a pain in my ass.

332 > Friend-poaching

It all started here, folks. This is where friend-poaching started to become socially acceptable, somehow. I think it was because all the swirling, blinking, ADD-inducing GIFs had us distracted. We didn't realize we were friending jerks who had no qualms about stealing our friends.

333 > No new notifications

Once upon a time you got e-mail notifications, letting you know when you had a new friend request, comment, or bulletin. Then, in a not-so-subtle ploy to get you to log in regularly to see if you've gotten anything new, MySpace ended that courtesy. But when you hate the site, you don't log in . . . unless you get an e-mail notification telling you to do so. MySpace, please meet rock and hard place. You'll be sitting in the middle seat on a flight with them to Australia.

Chapter 21

Blogs, Glorious Blogs: The Narcissistic Land of Live Journal and Blogger

334 > Only Perez Hilton "got it"

Diaries are supposed to be private, so why don't you keep this stuff to yourself? I do think there's a place for blogs (I would never talk down to Perez or Wonkette, for example), but I always thought the personal web diaries would die. Only, they haven't. And every person out there thinks they're going to get "discovered" with their blogs posting the ten things they want in a guy or stories of how lonely they are. I got news for you people—*everybody* is lonely. And while we all have our moments of being unapologetically pathetic, those are times we should really pick up the phone and call a friend.

335 > Don't you WANT to talk to your friends?

People say the great thing about personal blogs is they help you keep your friends and family up to date on what you're doing. That's great, but do you remember the days when Aunt Gladys used to send out the photocopied yearly wrap-up each Christmas? Remember how everyone made fun of her? That's because she was doling out information without any regard for the person receiving it. It was a long, only slightly personal monologue, the precursor to the bloody blog.

336 > Is it *really* necessary to blog from your cell phone?

People do this! LiveJournal lets you do this. If blogs are actually about getting something off your chest and expressing yourself, can't you at least give a little bit of merit to what you post by writing about it on a real keyboard? By spell checking? You know, all that good stuff.

337 > For real? You're blogging about your cat? Again?!

What is it with people and their cats? Look, I live with two cats, so I don't hate cats, but I do tend to favor people who have other things to talk about besides cats. I don't want to see another photo of your cat. I just don't. If I want to see a photo of a cat, I will go to icanhascheezburger.com. I won't go to a site of a single cat-lover who models her life after *Sex and the City*, minus the friends, the fun, and the style.

338 > Mommy bloggers

Everyone has a dream. And for every mother who blogs, her dream is to be Dooce. Well, honey, Dooce got something you don't got. Dooce has an outrageous sense of humor and the ability to create drama, entertainment, and suspense where there would otherwise be none. Dooce also works her skinny ass off by posting a bazillion times a week. (Don't know her? Go to *www.dooce.com* and see for yourself!) A random photo of your kid and commentary on how much he likes strained peas does not a Dooce make. Really, you're boring the hell out of me.

339 > Bloggers as "serious journalists" and the readers that take them seriously

Suddenly everyone is a journalist and, as honorary members of the Fourth Estate, there to protect the proletariat from an oppressive dictator government. Even people who didn't get past a fourth-grade education. Suddenly, opinions are being revered as serious journalism and real journalists are being frowned upon for either taking too much time to delve deep and report accurately or for reporting in real time and getting their facts wrong. And usually the journalists are being lambasted by the bloggers, who wouldn't know the meaning of the word "unbiased" if it poked them in the eye.

340 > Blogrolls, but I don't want to blogroll your stupid site!

I know that the more sites that blogroll you the higher your Google ranking will be. So, I suppose I understand your tendency to be completely indiscriminate when it comes to blogrolling. But I don't want to hear it. Don't tell me that you'll scratch my back if I scratch yours. I hate your site and I'm not going to blogroll it. And to blogroll it doesn't even make sense. My site is a cooking site; I'm not going to blogroll an anti-gun-control site. You moron.

341 > Hate comments

Oh, this makes me sad. I think her taste in home décor is atrocious too, but I don't want to make her feel bad about it. At least not on her own blog. Come on people, I know they're airing their dirty laundry for all to see, so they're kind of asking for it, but can't you just be nice? There's no need to post nasty comments on someone's blog. It doesn't make me commiserate with you; it makes me think you're a really mean-spirited a-hole. At least, if you're not going to be nice, can't you just go out with your friends, have a beer, and make fun of people behind their backs? Come to think of it, you've gotten me so bummed out about humanity, I kind of want to protect her and her furniture from the likes of you.

342 > LiveJournal's multitiered geekery

While personal diary blogs are universally annoying, LiveJournal blogs take narcissism to dizzying heights. Known for drama and teenage angst, Live-Journal is also a geek's paradise where legions of role-players can get their jollies out in new ways. Like connection to thousands of other bloggers who like to make *Harry Potter* characters have sex with each other. Seriously, LiveJournal: where have you been all my life?

343 > Always bringing me down

If you don't know constant outages, lost posts, slowness, and other forms of technical mayhem, you don't know LiveJournal. It's kind of what Live-Journal is famous for and how it's made its mark. But don't be so down on LiveJournal. What else can you expect if you share your servers with a million teenagers frantically refreshing their "friends lists"?

344 > But if you're going to blog . . .

At least let's have a blog site that gives the options to categorize your posts. LiveJournal offers no categories. That's right, folks. You have to keep a separate journal if you want to give your readers an ability to read only stuff that interests them. I want to write some entries in Russian, but do not want to have a separate journal for that. Also, some of my readers might be interested in my photos, but not in what I think about LiveJournal.

345 > Geekageddon

The thing geeks love about LiveJournal is how easily "trolls" can be banished and how they can create a high school hierarchy that lets them be at the top of the pack. They can engineer high drama through friend list manipulation and they can banish anyone who doesn't sufficiently flatter their super-mutant enhanced egos through sycophantic praise.

Chapter 22

LinkedIn: More Inflated Egos and False Expertise

346 > Pillaging of contacts

When you pillage my contacts it doesn't make me want to recommend you; it makes me want to smack you. This is not connecting. And how do you figure being connected to my massage therapist is going to get you a job when you're a "compliance expert"? You know what—not only is it not going to get you a job, it's going to make me damn sure to give you a crappy recommendation.

347 > Everyone here is unemployed

Color me confused. So, LinkedIn is allegedly a site to help you network for a job, right? But everyone here seems to be unemployed. Call me dense, but when everyone on LinkedIn seems to be unemployed, how are they going to help me find a job?

348 > Join a group, get 10,000 e-mails you couldn't care less about.

The thing about online social networking is that you find out every person you used to look up to, respect, and admire is just as desperate as you are.

Somehow I assumed LinkedIn would be more formal or—dare I say—professional? But professionalism seems to go out the window when it comes to group discussions. It's like a spam fiesta, with people so overeager to show their knowledge on a particular subject that you don't want to listen to any of them.

349 > Social networking gurus' unreasonable fervor for LinkedIn

I have never gotten a job from LinkedIn. Never. And no one I know has either. Maybe it's the circles I run in, but the only people who claim to have gotten a job through LinkedIn had so many professional accomplishments to their name that I sincerely doubt their LinkedIn account is what got them hired. But social networking gurus love this site and will cram it down your throat at any opportunity. It just looks like an online rat race to me: a place where people do their best to be noticed but just end up looking overeager.

350 > Nowhere to hide

I know there's a way to hide my profile from my boss, but in the three years I've been on LinkedIn I haven't been able to find it. I know this because my boss asked me about my profile. A woman who doesn't know the difference between Twitter and Twister sure as hell is going to get the wrong impression when she sees your LinkedIn profile posting all of your recent accomplishments, with references to how they make you employable to a prospective company. Actually, she's not getting the wrong impression at all, but don't tell her that.

351 > Sometimes it's necessary to lie; LinkedIn totally outed me

Let's be truthful here, people; who hasn't beefed up their resume a little bit to get that dream job? So, maybe I didn't *lead* the team that launched a new website, but I did fetch coffee and take a whole bunch of notes at the meetings. I did stuff! And let me tell you, without that coffee there would have been a whole slew of people falling asleep—so when I say I "helped generate ideas," it's only a little bit of a stretch. The whole point of a resume is to tell people how awesome you are. I mean, eHow even has a whole entry dedicated to faking your resume. And if eHow says it's okay, it has to be okay. Right?

352 > It's suddenly okay to use people? WTF?

Once upon a time, relationships were communicative. Yes, even professional relationships. If you had lost touch with a boss and really needed his recommendation, you would pick up the phone, catch up for a bit, and then talk about your professional needs. I have been in more situations than I can count where a person I know marginally asks me to introduce them to someone I kind-of know who maybe knows someone I don't know at all. So, yeah: I know I only kind-of know you, but could you give a glowing recommendation to your ex-boss for this guy I met at a party last week? Don't know about his sales skills, but you wouldn't believe what that guy can do with some Jägermeister and an ice luge.

> **Red Flag for Failure**
>
> Encourage people to use their friends.

353 > In cyberspace, networking will cost ya!

Network is supposed to be about bringing people together, forming bonds so that they can share resources, joining hands and singing Kumbaya. . . . But for LinkedIn networking seems to be about baiting me to upgrade to a paid account. They dangle the carrot: "15 more people checked out your account" but you're left in the dark if you don't fork over the dough. Well, it ain't gonna happen LinkedIn and, since it seems like everyone on your site is unemployed, looks like you're not going to hit your projected revenue this year.

Chapter 23

Social Networking Freaks and Geeks

354 > I need a secretary to keep track of it all

They've got you Twittering, and YouTubing, and Facebooking, and then you're on LinkedIn for business reasons, and you keep your MySpace account so you can keep track of music, and you have a Flickr account for photos, and a WordPress account so you can start a brilliant blog that Oprah will love and that will help you quit your job. And then you join MyLife and Classmates because you might miss that friend from high school who moved to Nebraska. But that's not enough. It's never enough, because now people want you to join FriendFeed and then everyone is nudging you because you don't have time to tweet because you still don't get the point of Twitter.

355 > Tribe.net

The good thing about Tribe is that they actually tried to get you to meet people. Basically, it's a band of hippies on the Internet inviting you to all their parties. Too good to be true, right? The bad thing about Tribe is that it tried to actually make social networking social as opposed to being a way to amp up our meta-self-awareness to a frightening degree. That's right: the site that allows you to hear what kind of soup people are eating and what color socks the girl from study group is wearing makes more sense to the masses. Oh, the insanity.

356 > You didn't know how bad people smelled until you actually met them in person

Tribe is a lot of hippies. Hippies are, by and large, stinky. Don't forget that. Your monitor may smell like lilacs with a hint of Windex but, chances are, the hippie you met off of Tribe will not.

Red Flag for Failure

Create a site that is modeled on real interaction as opposed to geekery.

357 > The whole site went silent during Burning Man

Wow, this is like a scene from *I Am Legend*. Where did all the hippies go? So this is what the world would be like without hippies? Cleaner, more articulate, and much better music. Quick, hand me that Big Mac before they get back.

358 > MyLife.net

Why does Reunion.com keep changing its name? I couldn't even find my freaking account and then one day I figured out that it's not Reunion.com anymore. It's MyLife.com. Because no one went on the site to have a reunion with anyone, now we all have to hear Bon Jovi running through our heads every time we log in. Which is never, so I don't know why I'm complaining.

> **Red Flag for Failure**
>
> Change the name of your site every fifteen seconds.

359 > Friggin' Flickr

If you tell me how to crop my photos one more time I'm going to hunt you down and throw a pie in your face. Flickr is hands-down the best site for storing photos, and the best site for finding opinions that you never asked for. It must be somewhere in the terms of service that if you open a Flickr account you suddenly become Henri Cartier-Bresson and have a right to critique everyone's photos.

360 > The slow stumble of FriendFeed

The point of FriendFeed is to aggregate all of your social networking sites—Facebook, Twitter, Flickr, Amazon wishlist, StumbleUpon—into one nice organized information feed. So it's kind of like a tool to organize the tools in an incredibly messy garage. But I gotta tell you, an eight-hour update delay just isn't working for me. I suppose this format would work fine for people who only checked in every day or so, but do you really think people who sign up for FriendFeed check accounts that infrequently?

361 > FriendFeed: Nobody's on it

While Mashable is touting FriendFeed as the next big thing, I only have four friends on it right now. Since it's half aggregator and half social networking service, it can hardly be touted as useful in the latter. No, rather it's just one more place for me to visit. Just one more way for the Internet to slobber all over me and make me feel confused.

362 > Just another social network

FriendFeed isn't just an aggregator, it is actually another social network. Your friends have to be on it for you to follow them and they have to friend you in order for everything to work. It also allows for commenting on everything that shows up in your feed. So, while it's great that it pulls together all of your online activity into one convenient package, it fragments conversations. While that works for some, it feels more like tiny pools of linguistic spittle to me.

363 > Oh God, FriendFeed groups?

For real? How many groups can one person become a member of before they cease to care?

364 > Overly simplistic design

I get the whole simplicity thing. I really do, but there comes a time when things are so simplified they cross over into "dumbed down" and become unusable. If you were to visit the FriendFeed home page with fresh eyes for the very first time, I'm sure you'd have no idea what you're supposed to do on the site. It just looks like a very clean, very useless page with not too much going on. Next?

365 > Apps, apps, and more apps for the FriendFeeders

Just what we need. Another social networking site that requires third-party applications in order for it to have any real use. Don't we already have this? And don't we call it Twitter?

Sources

Independent.ie / *www.Independent.ie*

ITBusiness.ca / *http://ITBusiness.ca*

MarketingVOX / *www.marketingvox.com*

Pew Internet & American Life Project / *www.pewinternet.org*

Twitionary / *http://twitter.com/Twitionary*

The Unofficial Facebook Privacy Group / *www.facebook.com*

The Urban Dictionary / *www.urbandictionary.com*

About the Author

Janelle Randazza has Friendstered, Facebooked, and Twittered her way into a writing career where she turns out articles on everything from Warcraft Widows (*Boston Phoenix*) to Sicilian winemaking (*Yankee Magazine*). She is also a semi-professional music groupie, but avoids stalking her favorite bands on MySpace. She recently moved from the Boston area to Los Angeles.